Matter and Mind

Also by SUBHASH KAK

The Architecture of Knowledge
The Nature of Physical Reality
The Astronomical Code of the Ṛgveda
The Gods Within
Computation in Ancient India
Mind and Self: Patañjali's Yoga Sūtra and Modern Science
The Prajñā Sūtra: Aphorisms of Intuition
The Wishing Tree
In Search of the Cradle of Civilization
The Aśvamedha
Arrival and Exile
The Loom of Time

Matter and Mind

The Vaiśeṣika Sūtra of Kaṇāda

Subhash Kak

Mount Meru Publishing

Library and Archives Canada Cataloguing in Publication

Kaṇāda
[Vaiśeṣikasūtra. English]
Matter and mind: the Vaiśeṣika Sūtra of Kaṇāda / [translation and commentary by] Subhash Kak.

Translated from Sanskrit.
Includes bibliographical references and index.
Issued in print and electronic formats.
ISBN 978-1-988207-13-1 (paperback).--ISBN 978-1-988207-14-8 (html)

1. Kaṇāda. Vaiśeṣikasūtra. 2. Vaiśeṣika--Early works to 1800. I. Kak, Subhash, 1947-, editor, translator II. Title. III. Title: Vaiśeṣikasūtra. English.

B132.V2K313 2016 181'.44 C2016-904262-6
C2016-904263-4

Published in 2016 by:
Mount Meru publishing
P.O. Box 30026
Cityside Postal Outlet PO
Mississauga, Ontario
Canada L4Z 0B6
Email: mountmerupublishing@gmail.com

ISBN 978-1-988207-13-1

Cover image: Pixabay (https://pixabay.com)

CONTENTS

PREFACE

Our ideas and theories are based in consciousness, yet science has no place for it. In our mind's eye, we see the universe as stars and planets in motion with us as specks of dust in the enormous expanse of space and time. We speak of principles of symmetry and information as fundamental to physical laws, but these are characteristics primarily of cognition, whereas our physics is based on things, their qualities, and their mutual interactions.

In biology one speaks of beauty as playing an important purpose through natural selection, but beauty can only exist in consciousness. We wish to describe the world through relationships of things, but these descriptions implicitly assume a being.

There is one unique system of physics that considers not only matter but also observers (and consciousness) and this system is described in the Vaiśeṣika Sūtra, which presents a conceptual representation of space, the gross visible matter composed of four different kinds of atoms, and sentient observers.

The originator of the Vaiśeṣika is Kaṇāda (sometimes also called Ulūka), who is believed to have lived around 600 BCE or not much later thereafter. The Vaiśeṣika is believed to precede the ancient system of the Nyāya, or logic, which is closely tied to it, and it is known to the physician Caraka who quotes it in his Sūtrasthāna. In both the Nyāya and the Vaiśeṣika, minds are not empty slates; the very constitution of the mind provides some knowledge of the nature of the world. The four means (pramāṇas) through which correct knowledge is acquired are direct perception, inference, analogy, and verbal testimony.

In my study of the Vaiśeṣika, I have become convinced that Kaṇāda is perhaps the greatest natural philosopher before Newton, if for nothing else than the breadth of his conceptual system. He considers symmetry arguments in relation to physical law, defines causality clearly, and anticipates much of Newton in his laws of motion. Further, he does something extraordinary by creating a formal system that includes space, time, matter, and observers and explaining how subjective experiences (qualia) arise.

Sadly, there are no contemporary studies of the Vaiśeṣika Sūtra exploring its physics content and the last major commentary on it, titled Upaskāra, was written by Śaṅkara Miśra in the 15th century. A manuscript of Upaskāra in Miśra's handwriting has a date corresponding to 1473 CE on it (Śāstri, 2002). Brajendranath Seal who wrote a general summary of Indian physics in 1915 quoted Śaṅkara Miśra extensively. More recent Vaiśeṣika studies have emphasized issues of interest to philosophers rather than to physicists (e.g. Halbfass, 1992; Chakrabarty, 2003; Kumar 2013). The tradition of seeing Nyāya and Vaiśeṣika as one larger philosophical school has continued to garner the most attention (as in Matilal, 1977) with the focus on logical and linguistic analyses of the sūtras.

The beginnings of this translation and commentary go back about ten years when I asked my pupil Roopa Narayan, who was then in the United States, to study it but she had to return to India and abandon the project after a few years. The final push for this translation and commentary was the request for an article on Indian physics for an encyclopedia which eventually grew to a size that it needed to be published as a book.

This study is not concerned with the history of the Vaiśeṣika and my purpose is to delve into Kaṇāda's system ignoring the modifications that were introduced by later commentators.

The introduction is a preliminary analysis of the Vaiśeṣika. As one can see, the sūtras have much of relevance for the contemporary debates on mind and matter, and how sentient beings make sense of the universe and have agency in a world governed by laws.

Subhash Kak
Stillwater, Oklahoma
May 26, 2016

INTRODUCTION

The Upaniṣads (e.g. Taittirīya and Śvetāśvatara) present the doctrine of five elements (*mahābhūtas*) that are named earth (*pṛthivī*), water (*āpas*), fire (*tejas*), air (*vāyu*), and ether (*ākāśa*), that represent mass, fluidity, light and fire, gaseousness, and the substratum for vibration. It is explained that since the same substance changes its phase based on heat or cold, the elements of each are present in every substance.

Since earth, water, fire, air, and ether are loaded words, from now one we will generally use the Sanskrit terms for the elements. The Chāndogya Upaniṣad says this of the relationship between the elements of the universe: From this self (ātman), ākāśa arose; from ākāśa vāyu; from vāyu tejas; from tejas āpas; from āpas pṛthivī. In the Śānti Parvan in the Mahābhārata, the sequence of dissolution of the physical universe is as follows: Under extreme heat, pṛthivī becomes āpas, then tejas, then vāyu, then ākāśa, then space, then mind, then time, then energy, and finally universal consciousness.

The transformation sequence of the elements clearly shows that atoms appear from space and prior to that from consciousness. Evolution and transformation is one of the basic characteristics of the system of five elements. Indian physics is a logical system building upon this doctrine that strives to analyze physical reality in a surprisingly comprehensive manner.

General ideas of evolution of the physical universe and how elementary atoms arise out of the subtle tanmātras, explaining the origin of the atoms of Vaiśeṣika, are part of the Sāṅkhya system and are also touched upon in Vedānta texts. Astronomy siddhāntas provide us further information on how motion was considered in astronomy (e.g. Burgess, 1860; Shukla and Sarma, 1976). Additional scattered references of relevance to physical ideas are to be found in the Purāṇas, the Yoga Vāsiṣṭha and the Mahābhārata and of chemical ideas in the Āyurvedic literature.

It should be stressed that Indian physical and chemical sciences were not merely theory. Chemical substances were studied on their own for their usefulness in medicine, textiles, food products, dyes, agriculture and metallurgy. These substances were also seen as arising out of different combinations of elementary atoms (Ray, 1909). Chemistry was called Rasāyana Śāstra, Rasa-Vidyā, and Rasatantra, which roughly mean 'science of liquids.' The term for a chemical concoction was rasa and the chemist was referred to as a Rasajña and Rasa-tantra-vid.

Careful observation (in astronomy, agriculture, chemistry, and medicine) and abstract thought (in grammar, cosmology), interconnected by unifying ideas, characterize these scientific models. The measurements are in terms of elaborate systems of times, lengths, and weights. Time was measured using different kinds of clocks and gnomons. The measures of time are defined in the following manner in the Purāṇas and the Arthaśāstra: 15 nimeṣa = 1 kāṣṭhā; 30 kāṣṭhā = 1 kalā; 30 kalā = 1 muhūrta; 30 muhūrta = 1 day-

and-night, and variants thereof in other texts (in one text 100 truṭi= 1 tatpara, and 30 tatpara=1 nimeṣa), and beyond this are cycles of yugas of increasingly larger periods that are billions of years long. There was a similarly systematic measurement of lengths with aṅgula (finger) being the base which went to 1 yojana in the scheme: 12 aṅgula= 1 vitasti; 16 vitasti= 1 dhanu (bow length); 1,000 dhanu = 1 yojana (with many other units in between). There were other units that looked at fractions of aṅgula. Rulers made from ivory were in use in the third millennium BCE. One such ruler calibrated to about 1/16 of an inch was found in Lothal.

Scholars have found that the Harappan measures are the same as the one in the historic period (Balasubramaniam and Joshi, 2008; Danino, 2008). The smallest weights were calibrated with respect to seeds of rice or wheat berry. Figure 1 presents a picture of standardized cubic stone weights from the third millennium BCE Harappan era from the Kot Diji Phase around 2800-2600 BCE. The first seven weights are in the binary sequence 1:2:4:8:16:32:64 (with some anomalous exceptions), where the unit corresponds to 0.856 grams; the most common weight being the 16 unit one. Next are the increments in a decimal system in multiples of 16 in the range 160, 320, and 640. Next are the weights 1,600, 3,200, 6,400, and 12,800. The Arthaśāstra describes standardized measures.

Apart from the study of motion, Indians also studied vibratory phenomena, acoustics, and transforming power of fire. It was known that lightning bolts had electricity and which was taken to be a property of the tejas atoms. Magnetism was also known and the Suśruta Saṃhitā 27 speaks of how a loose unbarbed arrow lodged in a wound with a broad mouth can be withdrawn by the use of a magnet (Bhishagratna, 1907). A compass consisting of an iron fish floating in a pan of oil is described. The attraction of a piece of iron to a magnet is mentioned in the epic poem Kumārasambhava 2.59 by the poet Kālidāsa.

Figure 1: Cubic weights from 2800-2600 BCE (Morley and Renfrew, 2010)

There are accounts of temples with levitating images as in Somnath, which was destroyed by Mahmud of Ghazni in 1025-1026. When the temple fell "the king directed a person to go and feel all around and above it with a spear, which he did but met with no obstacle. One of the attendants then stated his opinion that the canopy was made of loadstone [a magnetized rock], and that the idol was iron and that the ingenious builder had skillfully contrived that the magnet should not exercise a greater force on any one side -- hence the idol was suspended in the middle. When two stones were removed from the summit the idol swerved on one side, when more were taken away it inclined still further, until it rested on the ground." (Elliot and Dowson, 1876, volume 1, page 97)

Although Indian approach to physical reality is pragmatic, a central idea underlying its models is that language cannot describe reality completely. Descriptions are fundamentally incomplete and when stretched beyond normal boundaries they lead to logical paradox. Due to the limitation of language, experienced reality can never be described fully. Knowledge is of two kinds: the lower or dual; and the higher or unified. The lower knowledge is empirical and it concerns the world of objects and things that are subject to change and transformation, whereas the higher knowledge concerns the experiencing self.

Physics and chemistry are a part of lower knowledge. The unfolding of the universe is according to laws (*ṛta*) and the seemingly irreconcilable worlds of the material and the conscious are complementary aspects of the same transcendental reality. In a famous dialog in the Bhāgavata Purāṇa, the sage Nārada instructs that study of lower, empirical knowledge until one has realized its limitations is essential preparation for receiving higher knowledge.

Since the universe cannot arise out of nothing, it must be infinitely old. Since it must evolve, there are cycles of chaos and order or creation and destruction. The Ṛgveda speaks of the universe being infinite in size. A famous mantra speaks of how taking infinity out of infinity leaves it unchanged. This indicates that paradoxical properties of the notion of infinity were known. The world is also taken to be infinitely old. Beyond the solar system, other similar systems were postulated. An infinite size of the universe logically led to the acceptance of many worlds.

The following passage of Mahābhārata 12.182 speaks clearly of the infinite size of the universe in the following words: "The sky you see above is infinite. Its limits cannot be ascertained. The sun and the moon cannot see, above or below, beyond the range of their own rays. There where the rays of the sun and the moon cannot reach are luminaries which are self-effulgent and which possess splendor like that of the sun or the fire. Even these luminaries do not behold the limits of the firmament in consequence of the inaccessibility and infinity of those limits. This space which the very gods cannot measure is full of many blazing and self-luminous worlds each above the other." (Ganguly, 1990)

EARLY MATHEMATICS

The understanding of physical reality requires the application of mathematics, both in the abstract and numerical forms. Indian texts have many ill-understood mathematical allusions and they speak of large numbers at many places. The Yajurveda gives a sequence of powers of 10 going to 10^{12}. In the Vedic book called Śatapatha Brāhmaṇa (ŚB), there is a sequence speaking of different successive divisions of the year that amounts to $10{,}800\times15^6$ parts. Elsewhere the number of stars is given as 1.08×10^7. Other numbers are used symbolically.

A famous verse from the Īśa Upaniṣad speaks of "fullness" from which "fullness" arises and if "fullness" is subtracted from it "fullness" remains, which indicates that the Vedic authors had the intuition of the mathematical idea of infinity. Elsewhere, there is explicit mention of infinity as being uncountable.

Some stories in the texts have a mathematical basis. For example, the Maitrāyaṇīya Saṃhitā has the story of Manu with ten wives, who have one, two, three, four, five, six, seven, eight, nine, and ten sons, respectively. The one son allied with the nine sons, and the two sons allied with the eight, and so on until the five sons were left by themselves. They asked the father for help, and he gave them each a *samidh*, or "oblation- stick," which they used to defeat all of the other sons.

Since the ten sons did not ally with anyone, and the pairing of the others, except the five left over, is in groups of ten, the counting is in the base 10 system. In this mathematical story, the sticks help make the five stronger than the other 50. Perhaps this happens because each stick has a power of 10, and therefore the 5 now have a total power of 55 which vanquishes the 50. This could imply knowledge of the place value system if one conjectures that each oblation-stick is in the higher place value so that 50+5=55.

In ŚB, the total number of syllables in the Ṛgveda is said to be 432,000, equal to the number of muhūrtas in 40 years (each muhūrta = 48 minutes). The Yajurveda and the Sāmaveda together are taken to be another 432,000 syllables. An early index to the Ṛgveda due to Śaunaka states that the number of words in the book is 153,826, and this number is twice 76,913, which is a prime number. Since the mantras are in verses of two lines, one might expect that the number 76,913 is the more basic one and it was deliberately chosen. Likewise, the total number of verses in the Ṛgveda is 10522 = 2 × 5261, and 5261 is prime. But these two examples of primality could just be accidental, unless one could show that the Vedic authors actually knew this concept.

It appears that in the Vedic texts one can distinguish between numbers that are derived from observed phenomena and others that are ideal, or have an abstract basis. It is the latter numbers that are likely to be prime. It is due to the assumption of connections, *bandhu*, between the astronomical, the physical, and the elemental, which is central to Vedic thought, that many numbers are astronomical and related to the motions of the sun, moon, and the planets. Other numbers show up where the narrative transcends astronomy or physical structure and describes the Puruṣa, the Cosmic Man, as in *yantras*. These are non-astronomical and may be prime or have large prime factors.

Astronomical numbers in the Vedic texts are related to the 360 tithis of the lunar year, the 365 or 366 days of the solar year (or 371 or 372 tithis), the 27 or 28 nakṣatras, the 29 days of the month, numbers related to the divisions of the year, the planet orbits, synchronization periods for the lunisolar motions or planet motions, and so on. Another astronomical number is 108, the distance to the sun or the moon in terms of multiples of their respective diameters, and it figures in the earliest temple design. This number is also related to the nākṣatra year of 324 days (12 "months" of 27 lunar days). The earliest extant astronomy is in the Vedāṅga Jyotiṣa which has an internal date of the middle of the second millennium BCE and this provides an idea of the mathematics of that period.

Astronomical numbers are generally highly composite. The best examples are the cosmic cycle numbers, such as the longest cycle of 311,040,000 million years. Other numbers, which appear non-astronomical, may actually have an astronomical basis. For example, the 33 gods are likely related to the count of 27 nakṣatras, five planets, and the moon. Or consider Āyurveda physiology where the number of joints in the body (*marma*) is taken to be 107, a prime number. Its primality may not be the reason for its choice, because the 108 disks of the sun from the earth may have been taken to be mirrored in 108 links from the feet to the crown, and these 108 links will then have 107 joints. Some of the non-astronomical origin numbers may not be actual counts, but rather ideal counts and, therefore, the choice of the number as a prime becomes significant.

The Brāhmaṇas and the Śulbasūtras include several mathematical results that include the so-called Pythagoras theorem, many centuries before its later discovery in Greece. The other theorems of the Śulba include:

- The diagonals of a rectangle bisect each other.
- The diagonals of a rhombus bisect each other at right angles.
- The area of a square formed by joining the middle points of the sides of a square is half of the area of the original one.

- A quadrilateral formed by the lines joining the middle points of the sides of a rectangle is a rhombus whose area is half of that of the rectangle.

- A parallelogram and rectangle on the same base and within the same parallels have the same area.

- If the sum of the squares of two sides of a triangle is equal to the square of the third side, then the triangle is right-angled.

A variety of constructions are listed in the Śulba texts. Some of the geometric construction in these texts is based on algebraic solutions of simultaneous equations, both linear and quadratic. It appears that geometric techniques were used to solve many of these problems. These texts are familiar with fractions. The altars built according to the Śulba rules demonstrate knowledge of the lunar and the solar years. Since the shapes of the earth and sun altars were different (round and square, respectively), the representation of the year required constructions equating the area of the circle to that of the square.

THE PHYSICAL WORLD AND THE COSMOS

The Vedic texts present a tripartite and recursive world view. The universe is viewed as three regions of earth, space, and sky which in the human being are mirrored in the physical body, the breath (*prāṇa*), and mind. The processes in the sky, on earth, and within the mind are taken to be connected. This connection is a consequence of a binding (*bandhu*) between various inner and outer phenomena. At one level, it means awareness that certain biological cycles, such as menstruation, have the same period as the moon.

The connection between the outer and the inner cosmos is seen most strikingly in the use of the number 108 in Indian religious and artistic expression. It was known that this number is the distance from the earth to the sun and the moon in sun and moon diameters, respectively. This number was probably obtained by taking a pole of a certain height to a distance 108 times its height and discovering that the angular size of the pole was the same as that of the sun or the moon. The diameter of the sun is also 108 times the diameter of the earth, but that fact may not have been known to the Vedic sages (Kak, 2015).

Like astronomers in other cultures, Vedic astronomers discovered that the periods of the sun and the moon do not coincide. The Yajurvedic sage Yājñavalkya knew of a 95-year cycle to harmonize the motions of the sun and the moon and he also knew that the sun's circuit was asymmetric. Given the different periods of the planets, it became necessary to assume yet longer periods to harmonize their cycles. This ultimately led to the notion of mahāyugas and kalpas with periods of billions of years.

Although there were those who put Earth at the center of the solar system, a pure heliocentrism is to be found in the following statement in the Viṣṇu Purāṇa 2.8: "The sun is stationed for all time, in the middle of the day... The rising and the setting of the sun being perpetually opposite to each other, people speak of the rising of the sun where they see it; and, where the sun disappears, there, to them, is his setting. Of the sun, which is always in one and the same place, there is neither setting nor rising."

The rotation of the earth is inherent in the notion that the sun never sets that we find in the Aitareya Brāhmaṇa 2.7: "The [sun] never really sets or rises. In that they think of him 'He is setting,' having reached the end of the day, he inverts himself; thus he makes evening below, day above. Again in that they think of him 'He is rising in the morning,' having reached the end of the night he inverts himself; thus he makes day below, night above. He never sets; indeed he never sets." (Kak, 2016a)

The second millennium text Vedāṅga Jyotiṣa of Lagadha went beyond the earlier calendrical astronomy to develop a theory for the mean motions of the sun and the moon. An epicycle theory was used to explain planetary motions. But unlike the Greek epicycles, the Indian epicycles vary in size in the planetary circuit.

Astronomical texts called siddhāntas begin appearing sometime in the first millennium BCE. According to tradition there were 18 early siddhāntas of which only a few have survived (Burgess, 1860; Shukla and Sarma, 1976). Each siddhānta is an astronomical system with its own constants. In Āryabhaṭa mathematical theory, the earth was taken to spin on its axis and the periods of the planets were given with respect to the sun.

The Sāṅkhya system describes evolution at cosmic and individual levels. It views reality as being constituted of *puruṣa*, consciousness that is all-pervasive, motionless, unchangeable, without desire who at the individual level is the *sākṣin*, the witness, and *prakṛti*, which is the phenomenal world. Prakṛti is composed of three different strands (*guṇas* or characteristics) of *sattva, rajas*, and *tamas*, which are transparency, activity, and inactivity, respectively (Larson and Bhattacharya, 1987).

Evolution begins by puruṣa and prakṛti creating *mahat* (Nature in its dynamic aspect, as energy). From mahat evolves *buddhi* (intelligence) and *manas* (mind). From *buddhi* come individualized ego consciousness (*ahaṅkāra*) and the five *tanmātras* (subtle elements) of sound, touch, sight, taste, smell. From the manas evolve the five senses (hearing, touching, seeing, tasting, smelling), the five organs of action (with which to speak, grasp, move, procreate, evacuate), and the five gross elements (ether, air, fire, water, earth).

The evolution in Sāṅkhya is an ecological process determined completely by Nature. It differs from modern evolution theory in that it presupposes a cosmic intelligence and further beyond a universal consciousness. In reality, modern evolution also assigns intelligence to Nature in its drive to select certain forms over others as well as in the evolution of intelligence itself.

The Mahābhārata and the Purāṇas have material on creation and the rise of mankind. It is said that man arose at the end of a chain where the beginning was with plants and various kind of animals. In Vedic evolution the urge to evolve into higher forms is taken to be inherent in nature. A system of an evolution from inanimate to progressively higher life is taken to be a consequence of the different proportions of the three basic qualities of sattva, rajas, and tamas. In its undeveloped state, cosmic matter has these qualities in equilibrium. As the world evolves, one or the other of these becomes preponderant in different objects or beings, giving specific character to each.

REALITY AND WAYS OF KNOWING

Traditionally, there were six main schools of philosophy in India, each of which had its own approach to epistemology together with accepted means of cognition. There is agreement in these schools that as consciousness cannot be reduced to material phenomena, phenomenal reality has two aspects: one of material phenomena and the other of consciousness. Reality is dual at a phenomenal level but unitary at a deeper, transcendent level.

This transcendent reality can only be approached through a variety of unique and complementary perspectives. Like the room in space with its six different walls in which each window provides a different view, Indian philosophy has six *darśanas* (visions or "schools").

The mystery of reality may be seen through the perspectives of language (because at its deepest level it embodies structures of consciousness) and logic (Nyāya), physical categories (Vaiśeṣika), analysis of creation at the personal or the psychological level (Sāṅkhya), synthesis of experience (Yoga), structures of tradition (Mīmāṃsā), and cosmology (Vedānta). Each of these ways of seeing leads to different kinds of paradox that prepares the individual for the intuitive leap to the next insight in the ladder of understanding. Partial understanding obtained from the darśanas may appear contradictory, but that is how one becomes ready for a deeper intuition.

In the Vaiśeṣika sense perception and inference are valid means, whereas in the Sāṅkhya verbal testimony or scriptural authorities are additional means, and the Nyāya accepts comparison also as a means of valid cognition. The idea is that the knowledge furnished by one means must not be attainable by any other means, it should not be reducible to another, and it should not be contradicted by another means of cognition.

The tradition of logic, which developed in the background of the Vedic theory of knowledge, was divided by the historian Vidyābhuṣaṇa into three periods: ancient (up to 400 CE), medieval (400 CE – 1200 CE), and modern (1200 CE – 1850 CE). He saw the Nyāya Sutra of Akṣapāda Gautama (or Gotama) (c 550 BCE) as the foremost, if not the earliest, representative of the ancient period; Pramāṇa-samuccaya of Dignāga as representative of the medieval period; and Tattva-cintāmaṇi of Gaṅgeśa Upādhyāya as representative of the modern period. The medieval period produced many important glosses on the ancient period and much original thought. For example, Bhartṛhari (5th century CE) presented a resolution to the problem of self-referral and truth (Liar's paradox). In the modern period philosophers took up new issues such as empty terms, double negation, classification, and essences (Vidyābhuṣaṇa, 1990).

Gotama, the early teacher of the Nyāya, lists four factors involved in direct perception as being the senses (*indriyas*), their objects (*artha*), the contact of the senses and the objects (*sannikarṣa*), and the cognition produced by this contact (*jñāna*). *Manas*, the mind, mediates between the self and the senses. When the manas is in contact with one sensory organ, it cannot be so with another. It is therefore atomic in dimension. It is because of the nature of the mind that experiences are essentially linear, although quick succession of impressions may give the appearance of simultaneity. Sometimes Nyāya and Vaiśeṣika are considered a single school because the later tradition of Vaiśeṣika stressed inference over material properties.

Indian epistemology acknowledges error of cognition. The final test of such theories is the application to everyday experience. Since false theories and cognitions can affect one's understanding of reality and one's response to it, a kind of a relative truth may be ascribed to them.

The Sanskrit term for epistemology is *prāmāṇyavāda* (literally being established by proof). It deals with *prameya* or the object of cognition, *pramā* or *pramiti* which is the cognition itself, and *pramātṛ* or the subject that cognizes. A distinction is made between knowledge as *jñāna*, which is experience, and representation of it as *vijñāna* that can only approximate *true* knowledge. Self-knowledge comes through intuition which stands outside the subject-object dichotomy. Understanding proceeds in a paradoxical manner by the contemplation of the self through the self or, in Sanskrit terminology, the ātman through the ātman.

A later Nyāya philosopher recognizes four kinds of perception: sense perception, mental perception, self-consciousness, and yogic perception. Self-consciousness is a perception of the self through its states of pleasure and pain. In yogic perception, one is able to comprehend the universe in fullness and harmony.

A SUMMARY OF THE VAIŚEṢIKA SYSTEM

Kaṇāda in his sutras enumerates real entities that are apprehensible by the mind of the observer who is central to his world. These are the building blocks of Kaṇāda's world described through their guṇas (qualities) and karman (motion).

The Vaiśeṣika system has categories not only for space-time-matter but also for qualities related to perception of matter. It starts with six categories (*padārthas*) that are nameable and knowable. Nothing beyond these six fundamentals is necessary, because they are sufficient to describe everything in the universe from concrete matter to the abstract atom.

The six categories are: *dravya* (substance), *guṇa* (quality), *karman* (motion), *sāmānya* (universal), *viśeṣa* (particularity), and *samavāya* (inherence). An additional category of *abhāva* (negation) was added by some later scholars with the claim that these seven exhaust all aspects of reality. In this study, we argue that six is the appropriate number based on a fundamental consideration.

The first three of these have objective existence and the last three are a product of intellectual discrimination. Universals (*sāmānya*) are recurrent generic properties in substances, qualities, and motions. Particularities (*viśeṣa*) reside exclusively in the eternal, non-composite substances, that is, in the individual atoms, souls, and minds, and in the unitary substances ether, space, and time. Inherence (*samavāya*) is the relationship between entities that exist at the same time, permanently and inseparably. It is the binding amongst categories that makes it possible to synthesize experience. In later descriptions of the system a seventh category of "non-existence" is added.

Of the six categories, the basic one is that of substance and the other five categories are qualities associated with the substance. Observers belong to the system in an integral fashion for if there were no sentient beings in the universe there would be no need for these categories.

There are nine classes of substances (*dravya*), some of which are non-atomic, some atomic, and others all-pervasive. The non-atomic ground is provided by the three substances of ether (*ākāśa*), space (*dik*), and time (*kāla*), which are unitary and indestructible; earth (*pṛthivī*), water (*āpas*), fire (*tejas*), and air (*vāyu*) are atomic composed of indivisible, and indestructible atoms (*aṇu*); self (*ātman*), which is the eighth, is omnipresent and eternal; and, lastly, the ninth, is the mind (*manas*), which is also eternal but of atomic dimensions, that is, infinitely small. The consideration of self and mind as independent of physical substances makes this system a precursor to psychophysical parallelism that is the foundation of the Copehagen Interpretation of quantum theory.

Manas in other Indian systems is considered a kind of a sense-organ. Caraka in the Śarīrasthāna of the Caraka Saṃhitā speaks of the *kriyāvattva* (agency) of the manas. The notion of the eternality of the manas is paradoxical since that is where the eternality of the ātman squares with the transitoriness of the physical body and depending on the point of view, the mind is mortal when considering its ground but eternal when considering the agency of the ātman projected through it.

The basic atoms of pṛthivī, āpas, tejas, and vāyu will be represented by P, Ap, T, and V, respectively. The eternality of the atoms is true only under normal conditions. During creation and destruction, the atoms are created in a sequence starting with ākāśa and in a reverse sequence in the end of the world. The standard sequence of evolution of the elements is V→T→Ap→P, although sometimes it also written as T→V→Ap→P.

Air is generally mentioned as the medium for the transmission of sound, but a more subtle sound that pervades the universe requires the more abstract vāyu. The ordinary molecules of matter have all the basic atoms present in them. The interactions of the atoms are governed by four different forces: P interacts with all the four, Ap with 3, T with 2, and V with 1.

Scholars of the Vaiśeṣika who wish to reconcile modern physics and the atomic elements consider these to be proton, electron, photon, and neutrino, respectively. Their logic is that since the protons (and related neutrons) provide overwhelming portion of the mass of a substance pṛthivī = proton; when electronic bonds break, the substance becomes a liquid, therefore āpas = electron; tejas (light or fire) is obviously photon; and vāyu is neutrino for it is associated with the decay of the neutron into a proton (of course, this is speculative projection). The sutras have generally been interpreted to mean that only P and Ap have mass (Potter, 1997; pages 212 and 278).

This issue of mass is addressed by Śaṅkara Miśra in the Upaskāra who explains that T and V do not have mass for they do not interact gravitationally. But since the main characteristic of V is touch which is localized, one could argue that it should also have mass associated with it.

The atoms of ordinary earth, water, fire and air are different from the elementary atoms and this difference arises out of the different ways the fundamental atoms of materiality, P, Ap, T, V, combine with each other in different arrangements.

The four atoms are a function of four subtle elements called Ru (*rūpa*), Ra (*rasa*), Ga (*gandha*), and Sp (*sparśa*), corresponding to form, taste, odor, and contact. Symbolically, we may summarize this in terms of the following expressions:

$$P : \phi_1(Ru, Ra, Ga, Sp)$$
$$Ap : \phi_2(Ru, Ra, Sp)$$
$$T : \phi_3(Ru, Sp)$$
$$V : \phi_4(Sp)$$

Molecules that are comprised of many atoms may be represented by

$$Molecule : \varphi(P_m, Ap_n, T, V)$$

with mass equal to $mMass(P) + nMass(Ap)$ if it is accepted with the tradition that T and V do not possess mass.

It is postulated that distinguishing characteristics and motion are essential for the classification of matter. Space and time are identified through motion of matter or the sun. Of the substances, four (earth, water, fire, and air) are material (that is consisting of atoms) and capable of motion whereas five others (time, space, ether, ātman, and mind) are non-material and, therefore, no motion may be associated with them. It is significant that ātman is listed before mind, suggesting that it is the medium through which mind's apprehensions are received. The atoms of earth, water, fire and air are different and this difference arises out of the different ways the fundamental atom of materiality combines with itself in different arrangements.

The examination of the various parts of the Vaiśeṣika system reveals that its observables arise through the effect of motion in a consistent manner. As is true of other systems, this system leads to its own paradoxes. Yet, it offers a comprehensive and scientific view of the universe beginning with gross visible matter all the way up to the subtle invisible mind.

The atom is indivisible because it is a state for which no measurement can be attributed. What cannot be measured cannot be further divided and it cannot be spoken of as having parts. The motion the atom possesses is non-observable and it may be viewed as an abstraction in a conventional sense. Space and time are the two lenses through which matter is observed and they form the matrix of universe.

Normally, there is conservation of matter, but in extreme conditions, matter gets transformed into energy. Kaṇāda presents an opposition between *aṇu* and *mahat*, where the latter represents multiplicity or as something that pervades everywhere and may thus have been visualized as a wave.

When the universe ceases to be at the end of the cosmic cycle, matter is not annihilated; rather, it reaches a quiescent state where its atoms have no extrinsic motion and so become invisible, which appears very similar to the conception of the state of the giant atom at the beginning of cycle of creation. The lack of motion represents a cessation of time, because time is a measure of change.

In the epistemology of the Vaiśeṣika, it is possible to obtain knowledge due to the agency of ātman or self. Without the self, matter by itself cannot be sentient.

We now summarize the contents of the Vaiśeṣika Sūtra of Kaṇāda, which is a book of just over 370 verses in 10 chapters, where each chapter has two sections. Calling physical law *dharma*, the first chapter defines and discusses three categories of substance, attribute, and action. The second chapter describes the nine substances. The third chapter deals with the self and the mind.

The first part of the fourth chapter speaks of the eternality of atoms and how sensory perception leads to knowledge. The second part of the fourth chapter deals with the composition of bodies. The fifth chapter deals with action, and the sixth chapter deals with the discipline that facilitates acquisition of knowledge.

The seventh chapter elaborates on atomicity and further discusses the nature of ether, mind, space and time. The eighth and ninth chapters describe various types of cognition and negation, with the latter also distinguishing between *sat* and *asat*. The tenth chapter discusses cause.

KAṆĀDA'S LAWS

Kaṇāda's laws are an important component of the Vaiśeṣika physics. It is best to compare them to the corresponding laws of classical physics. Newton considered space and time to be absolute without explaining what that means. Newton's three laws of motion are: 1. An object remains in the state of rest or motion unless acted upon by force; 2. Force equals mass times acceleration; 3. To every action there is an equal and opposite reaction. For comparison, we begin with certain propositions of Kaṇāda that illustrate his system and then present the sūtras that describe physical laws related to motion. Note that Kaṇāda's atoms are in perennial motion and so he distinguishes between internal and outer motions of an object.

Principle 1. कर्म कर्मसाध्यं न विद्यते ॥१।१।११॥

karmaṃ karmasādhyaṃ na vidyate ‖1.1.11‖

From motion, new motion is not known.

Principle 2. कारणाभावात्कार्याभावः ॥१।२।१॥

kāraṇābhāvātkāryābhāvaḥ ‖1.2.1‖

In the absence of cause, [there is] absence of motion.

Principle 3. सामान्यं विशेष इति बुद्ध्यपेक्षम् ॥१।२।३॥

sāmānyaṃ viśeṣa iti buddhyapekṣaṃ ‖1.2.3‖

The [properties of] universal and particular are associated with the mind.

Principle 4. सदिति यतोद्रव्यगुणकर्मसु सा सत्ता ॥१।२।७॥

saditi yatodravyaguṇakarmasu sā sattā ॥1.2.7॥

Existence is [self-defined]. [Thus,] dravya, guna, and karman are sattā (potential).

Principle 5. सदकारणवन्नित्यम् ॥४।१।१॥

sadakāraṇavannityam ॥4.1.1॥

Existence is uncaused and eternal (*nitya*).

The principles have universal applicability. For example, the idea of symmetry is included in the principle of *nitya*, and Kaṇāda explains the roundness of the atom by this principle. The direct statement of causality in Principle 2 is remarkable. Now I present what may be called Kaṇāda's Laws of Motion.

Law 1. संयोगाभावे गुरुत्वात् पतनम् ॥५।१।७॥

saṃyogābhāve gurutvāt patanam ॥5.1.7॥

In the absence of conjunction, gravity [causes objects to] fall.

Law 2a. नोदनविशेषाभावान्नोर्ध्वं न तिर्य्यग्गमनम् ॥५।१।८॥

nodanaviśeṣābhāvānnordhvaṃ na tiryyaggamanam ||5.1.8||

In the absence of a force, there is no upward motion, sideward motion or motion in general.

Law 2b. नोदनादाद्यमिषोः कर्म तत्कर्मकारिताच्च संस्कारादुत्तरं तथोत्तरमुत्तरञ्च ||५।१।१७||

nodanādādyamiṣoḥ karma tatkarmakāritācca saṃskārāduttaraṃ tathottaramuttarañc ||5.1.17||

The initial pressure [on the bow] leads to the arrow's motion; from that motion is momentum, from which is the motion that follows and the next and so on, similarly.

Law 3. कार्य्यविरोधि कर्म ||१।१।१४||

kāryyavirodhi karma ||1.1.14||

Action (kārya) is opposed by reaction (karman).

This list above is a somewhat arbitrary arrangement of Kaṇāda's propositions. The first law is effectively equivalent to Newton's first law for due to Principle 2 the object will either continue to be at rest or in state of motion in the absence of action (including gravitation). The second law, in two parts, falls short, although it has something additional regarding potential. What is missing is an explicit definition of mass in relation to force, although mass is otherwise an element of the exposition. Kaṇāda's third law is identical to Newton's third law.

Most of the early expositions of Vaiśeṣika that followed Kaṇāda's sutras are lost. Perhaps this happened due to the high prestige of the commentary on the sutras titled Padārtha-dharma-saṅgraha by Praśastapāda of the fifth or sixth century CE. Other important scholars associated with this tradition include Candramati, Vyomaśiva, Udayana, and Śaṅkara Miśra, the author of the influential commentary Upaskāra (15th Century CE) (Matilal, 1977; Potter, 1997). The ideas of Vaiśeṣika were further elaborated by scholars of other darśanas. Important contributions to the discussion on the nature of atoms were made by Vyāsa (~4th century) and Vācaspati Miśra (9th or 10th century) who wrote commentaries on the Yoga Sūtra (Prasad, 1912). Many of the commentaries that followed focused on philosophical questions related to inference rather than underlying physical conceptions and these are not of interest to us in this study.

The ideas of the Vaiśeṣika have also been elaborated within the many schools of Vedānta (in their discussion of physics they are identical) that has influenced modern physics in many ways. Nikola Tesla was inspired to look for methods of harnessing energy from matter and space after learning of the transformation of ākāśa and other elements into energy (during dissolution) from Swami Vivekananda in a meeting in 1896. But he was unable to find the mass to energy equivalence relation (Nikhilananda, 1953).

According to the well-known biography of Schrödinger by Moore, philosophical ideas of Vedānta helped Schrödinger discover the key notion of quantum mechanics that the state function is a sum of all possibilities. Moore adds that in their development of the theory "Schrödinger and Heisenberg and their followers created a universe based on superimposed inseparable waves of probability amplitudes. This new view would be entirely consistent with the Vedantic concept of All in One." (Moore, 1987)

Now the Vaiśeṣika system is presented in terms of the main propositions on motion and force and ensuing inferences. The propositions below sometimes paraphrase the more formal translation that follows in the later chapters.

Categories, substances, and principles

Proposition 1.1. The six categories sufficient to construct the ontology of physical reality are: *dravya* (substance), *guṇa* (quality), *karman* (motion), *sāmānya* (universal), *viśeṣa* (particularity), and *samavāya* (inherence). (VS 1.1.4)

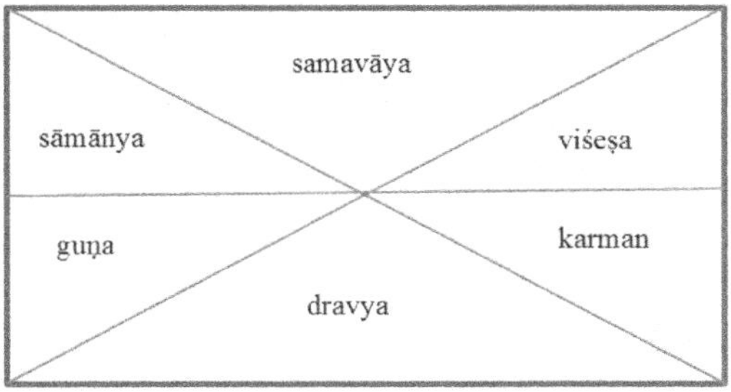

The six ontological categories (padārthas)

Proposition 1.2. There exist nine classes of *dravya* (substance) which are the five physical elements pṛthivī (earth), āpas (water), tejas (fire), vāyu (air), and ākāśa, kāla (time), dik (space), ātman (consciousness), and manas (the mind) of the observer. (VS 1.1.5)

Ākāśa endows space with its properties of vibration, and the capacity to generate and store energy.

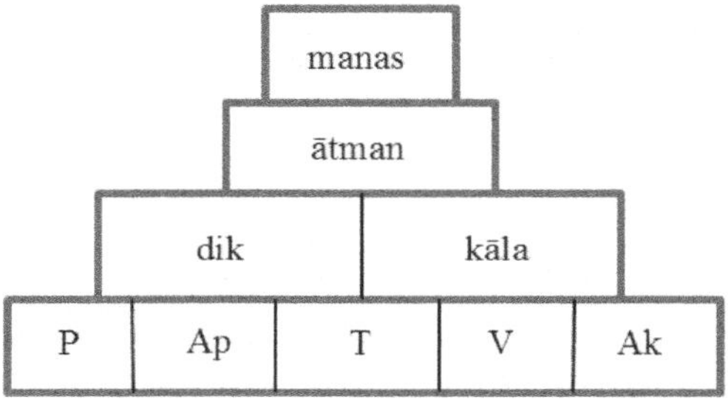

The nine dravyas (substances): P: pṛthivī; Ap: āpas; T: tejas; V: vāyu; Ak: ākāśa

Proposition 1.3. The qualities (*guṇas*) associated with materiality are form, taste, odor, contact, number, measure, distinctiveness, conjunction, disjunction, otherness, non-otherness, intellect, and [internal states of the mind] such as pleasantness, unpleasantness, desire, aversion, effort, and so on. (VS 1.1.6)

The guṇas, therefore, relate to the observations made upon interaction with matter. The final measurement belongs to the space of the mind. One basic measure of matter is mass. Since the material substances (which exclude mind and consciousness) are atomic, the guṇas emerge out of different kind of arrangements of the atoms and their motions. From the point of observation, the guṇas are detected by means of motions of some pointers in appropriate measurement instruments or transitions to specific states of the mind.

Proposition 1.4. There exist following types of motion: rising, falling, contraction, expansion, and general motion (*gamana*). (VS 1.1.7)

Praśastapāda explains in his commentary that *gamana* includes all motions other than the four mentioned earlier. It will therefore include both displacement, rotation (*bhramaṇa*) and vibration (*spandana*). He explains that the motion at any instant is really one, but for convenience of analysis, the rotatory change of place is taken to be separate from the change of place in the downward direction.

The falling leaf driven by the wind may have rotatory and vibratory motions as well as a vertical downward motion (patana) at the same time. Although each leaf taken separately has only one motion or change of place at one point, from the point of view of the observer (*draṣṭā*), it is convenient to speak of the rotatory change of place as separate from the displacement in the downward direction. The atoms are assumed to have a fundamental vibratory motion associated with them.

Motions not due to contact are caused by the following:

1. Volition (*prayatna*) as in the movement of the hand;
2. Gravitation as in a falling body. Brahmagupta speaks of attraction (*ākarṣaṇa*) exercised by the earth on a

material body. The force of gravity may be counteracted by volition as in the holding up of the hand; or by momentum (*vega*) that keeps the flying arrow from falling;

3. Motion of fluids as in the downward flow in a stream (*syandan*). This is due to fluidity (*dravyatva*) but Śaṅkara Miśra points out that fluidity is only a concomitant condition and the efficient cause remains gravity that acts on the particles in the fluid;
4. Other motions, not due to material contact, include magnetic attraction or repulsion or capillary motion; others due to final cause are called *adṛṣṭa* (unseen).

Motions due to contact include the following:

1. Motion due to direct contact with a body exercising continued pressure (*nodana*). This includes motion of an object pushed or pulled by the hand, motion of the mud under heavy stones, motion of the arrow due to pressure exercised by the bow-string, motion of the bow-string due to the pressure of the elastic bow as it recovers its original shape, motion of clouds, balloons, sailing vessels and other vehicles under the impelling force of the wind;
2. Motion due to direct contact for an instant with a body that strikes and produces an impact (*abhighāta*); so this is technically force. If there is continued contact, the result is pressure (*nodana*);
3. Motion due to direct contact with an elastic body which exercises a moving force by means of its elasticity in the act of restitution of the original form. The force of

restitution in an elastic body is a kind of saṃskāra (persistent tendency);

4. Motion due to contact with a body which is itself in contact with another that possesses *vega* (momentum).

The force that produces the first motion leads to a saṃskāra (potential) or persistent tendency to motion which is the cause of the motion in the straight line. The saṃskāra is taken to last until the cessation of the motion. The force of the saṃskāra diminishes by doing work against a counteracting force and when the saṃskāra is in this way entirely destroyed, the moving body comes to rest. The *vega* (impressed motion) is counteracted by contact with tangible objects, including friction with the still atmosphere, as in the case of the arrow. Praśastapāda says that *vega* produces work in opposition to the resisting force and thereby becomes progressively weaker until it comes to an end.

Proposition 1.5. Potential, transitoriness, substance-carried effort, cause, universality and particularity are grounded on dravya, guṇa, and karman. (VS 1.1.8)

A dravya can generate another dravya. In other words, substances are not immutable. Similarly, qualities also undergo transformation. However, dravya and guṇa cannot inter-transform since they are different kinds of classes. Motion may be transformed to work within the substance through friction. The atoms have the capacity to change their molecular structure during transformation.

Since space and time are dravyas, it is not surprising that neither of these is taken to be absolute.

Proposition 1.6. From motion, [new] motion is not known. (VS 1.1.11)

This is Principle 1 of the Introduction. Since in VS 5.1.17, it is asserted that one physical motion leads to another physical motion, this proposition is regarding intrinsic motion and it represents a conservation principle. To be specific, it is the conservation principle related to linear and angular momentum. The deeper intuition behind this conservation law is homogeneity of space, which is explicitly a part of Kaṇāda's system.

Proposition 1.7. Action is opposed by reaction. (VS 1.1.14)

This was presented as Law 3 of the Introduction. This law makes it possible to compute how high a ball would bounce. The ball strikes the ground with a certain force and the ground opposes this with an equal force. The force that the ball exerts on the ground is equal to and in the opposite direction as the force of the ground on the ball.

There is no explicit mention in the commentaries on how this might be of application to objects floating in water. Indians were skilled in building boats and ships and, therefore, such an extension was probably known to marine engineers.

A substance is associated with motion, qualities, and co-inherence. Motion leads to conjunction, disjunction, and motion in a substance, but it is not the cause.

Proposition 1.8. Upward motion is conjunction of gravitation and effort (force). (VS 1.1.29)

Gravitation is due to the attraction of the body by the earth, to counteract which effort is needed that makes the body travel upwards.

Proposition 1.9. In the absence of cause there is an absence of effect. (VS 1.2.1)

This is Principle 2 of the Introduction. The converse is not always true, as in the next proposition, for different kinds of causes may cancel each other.

Proposition 1.10. From absence of motion no absence of cause is implied. (VS 1.2.2)

This indicates that motions (or reactions thereof) are to be added linearly. If the addition was not linear that would imply one motion affecting another which is forbidden by Proposition 1.6. Motions can also be decomposed into components.

Proposition 1.11. The properties of universal and particular are ascertained by the mind. (VS 1.2.3)

This was presented as Principle 3. This asserts that these properties are subjective. To this extent, physical theories are a construction of the mind and are a window of the deeper reality of consciousness.

Proposition 1.12. Substance, attribute, and motion appear out of potential. (VS 1.2.7)

This was presented at Principle 4 of the Introduction. Although physical reality is taken to be explainable in terms of motion alone, a deeper origin of it is in potential. In VS 1.2.5 it is stated that these categories are both universal and particular. The potential associated with motion is to be considered in the start of the motion, as also in the consideration of origins.

It is further stated that the property related to substance, attribute, and action arises out of their respective universals.

Praśastapāda regards karman (motion) as instantaneous in its simplest form, distinguishing it from *vega* (impressed motion, momentum) which is a persistent tendency (*saṃskāra*) that implies a series of motions.

Substances and their characteristics

Pṛthivī is taken to have the qualities of form, taste, touch, and smell; āpas has qualities of form, taste, touch, and viscidity; tejas has form and touch; and vāyu has touch.

Proposition 2.1. Pṛthivī and āpas have mass. (VS 2.1.1- VS 2.1.4)

Taste and smell are here seen to arise from mass, and the followers of the system have generally assumed that form and touch do not so arise, although Kaṇāda makes no specific mention of this. This represents a basic connection between specific objects and the corresponding qualia. The fluidity of tin, lead, iron, silver and gold arises through conjunction with tejas. The description of these qualities is to associate the modes of matter with different subjective states.

Śaṅkara Miśra in the Upaskāra in the commentary on 1.1.5 argues that since tejas and vāyu do not interact gravitationally they have no mass. The consideration of touch as being localized could be interpreted to mean that vāyu also has mass.

Proposition 2.2. Ākāśa does not have the measurable qualities of pṛthivī, āpas, tejas, and vāyu. (VS 2.1.5)

The element ākāśa is different from the other four elements, which have specific measurable properties that have been mentioned in earlier sutras. Vibration is a characteristic of ākāśa, but this element is not atomic. Praśastapāda explains that there are two kinds of vibration: syllabic (*varṇa*) that represents speech, and *dhvani*, which is fundamental vibration.

In the Vedānta texts, ākāśa is the first stage in the evolution of matter from its pre-matter state. Ākāśa gives off vāyu, which gives off tejas, and on to āpas and pṛthivī. "Ākāśa (ether) itself passes through two stages before the emanation of the sūkṣma-bhūta vāyu: (1) the motionless ubiquitous primordial matter-stuff (answering to the Sāṅkhya *bhūtādi*) called *purāṇam kham*; and (2) a subtile integration, the pure un-quintuplicated sūkṣma bhūta called *vāyuram kham*, answering to the Sāṅkhya tanmātra stage. It is this subtile ākāśa, in its tanmātric integration, i.e. in the derivative form, which is subject to an incessant *parispanda*. The gaseous stage of matter (the Vedantic vāyu) is indeed matter in a state of parispandic motion. The Sāṅkhya also conceives this parispanda to characterize every process and phenomenon of cosmic evolution." (Seal, 1915, page 121) Ākāśa is therefore like the potential that exists in the vacuum from which arise other particles.

Proposition 2.3. Not inhering in other substances, vāyu is said to be eternal. (VS 2.1.13)

Thus the substance vāyu is used in two ways, as air, and as field and it is in the latter sense that it is eternal. It is also taken to be additive (VS 2.1.14).

Proposition 2.4. By method of exhaustion, śabda is a mark of ākāśa. (VS 2.1.27)

The vibration in ākāśa can only be like a wave for such a vibration is supposed to pervade the universe.

The conservation of matter is a consequence of the indestructible atoms of which it is taken to be composed.

Praśastapāda explains in his discussion of dissolution of the universe that the potential that exist in structure is exhausted and atoms fall back to their raw form. This is seen most clearly in the conception of how dissolution takes place in the Mahābhārata (Śānti Parva, chapter 233):

> When the time comes for universal dissolution, a dozen Suns begin to burn. All things mobile and immobile on Earth first disappear merging into the elements, making it shorn of trees and plants, looking naked like a tortoise shell. Then water takes up the attribute of earth element -- that is, the earth element becomes fluid. With mighty

> billows and roars, it pervades space. Next, water is transformed into heat. Dazzling flames of fire now conceal the Sun, and space itself begins to burn in a vast conflagration. Next, heat is transformed to wind, which becomes greatly agitated. In its attribute of sound, it begins to traverse upwards and downwards and transversely in all ten directions. Next, wind is transformed into space, with its attribute of unheard or unuttered sound. Finally, space withdraws into Mind. The chain continues a bit further until merging into the Consciousness, which is the ground-stuff of reality. (Ganguly, 1990)

In creation, on the other hand, pure atoms of pṛthivī etc combine to form dyads, triads, and so on, until elements as we know them are formed and gross structure of matter emerges. All qualities except contact, disjunction, number, and separateness between two things occur in one thing at a time. Number, size, separateness, contact, disjunction, farness and nearness, weight or measure, instrumental fluidity, and impetus are generic qualities; others are specific.

Viscidity is the distinguishing characteristic of liquids, and it is responsible for cohesion and smoothness.

Proposition 2.5. Closeness, nearness, farness, simultaneity, delay, and quickness are time-identifiers. (VS 2.2.6)

Time is not absolute, for it is defined in relative terms. Space is also defined in relative terms (VS 2.2.10). Spatial separation can only apply to matter since eternal dravyas which are incapable of motion can neither be separated nor brought together. Although mind can move, it is invisible. Therefore all that remains in Kaṇāda's classification of dravyas is matter.

The separation is an identifier and the identification is with reference to the observing mind. It is also significant that the displacement of matter is observed relative to another piece of matter. Both space and time are characterized by their guṇa or attribute of paratva-aparatva or separated versus joined.

Proposition 2.6. From the dichotomy of true and false knowledge doubt arises. (VS 2.2.20)

If there are polarities (or oppositions) then doubt arises related to the specific value.

Cognition

Proposition 3.1. Sensory perceptions are products of more than just the sensory inputs. (VS 3.1.2)

Perceptions arising in the mind are different from the actual sensory inputs for they are actively constructed by the mind. Knowledge is obtained by the falsification of some other possibility. Activity and inactivity seen in one's own ātman has the same mark as that of others. This implies a universal ground for subjective experiences.

Proposition 3.2. The proximity of consciousness and the objects of the senses, and the existence or non-existence of knowledge is a mark of the mind (VS 3.2.1)

Proposition 3.3. The mind is substantive and eternal. (VS 3.2.2)

Proposition 3.4. From the non-simultaneity of volitions and from the non-simultaneity of knowledge one mind is implied. (VS 3.2.3)

Proposition 3.5. Ātman appears substantive and eternal. (VS 3.2.5)

Based on the universality of perception, it cannot be inferred in particularity. (VS 3.2.7)

Proposition 3.6. The existence of "I" (of such an intuition) in one's own consciousness and absence in others indicates the perception of a substance other than the material. (VS 3.2.14)

This indicates a location of the intuition in a non-physical space.

Eternality, symmetry

Proposition 4.1. Existence is uncaused and eternal. (VS 4.1.1)

Inherent structure is a consequence of symmetry. The existence in the effect follows from existence in the cause. (VS 4.1.3) The atoms are taken to have distinct kinds of motions which, when considered together with the combination of the atoms, lead to different kinds of matter.

Proposition 4.2. A substance with extension is perceived from the many substances in it as the substratum and from its qualities. (VS 4.1.6)

In spite of body and extension, vāyu is invisible owing to the absence of the impression of form. (VS 4.1.7) According to Praśastapāda, the class of number resides both in single things and collection of things.

Action

Proposition 5.1. In the absence of conjunction, the object falls by gravity. (VS 5.1.7)

Although the degree of gravitational force is not specified, the proposition implies that in the absence of gravity the object will continue to remain in its state of rest or motion.

Proposition 5.2. In the absence of force, there is no upward motion, sideward motion or general motion. (VS 5.1.8)

Proposition 5.3. In an arrow, particular conjunctions explain successive motions. (VS 5.1.16)

Proposition 5.4. The arrow's initial motion is caused by force that leads to motions created by successive potentials. (VS 5.1.17)

Proposition 5.5. In the absence of the potential, gravitation causes the arrow to fall. (VS 5.1.18)

The impact of the force and the conjunction of atoms results in the motion of the material substance. (VS 5.2.1) In the absence of action, liquids flow down due to gravitation. Fluidity is the mechanism of the flow. (VS 5.2.4)

Praśastapāda explains that fluidity is of two kinds: natural (*saṃsiddhika*) and instrumental (*naimittika*). Fluidity is a natural characteristic of water. When it freezes, its natural fluidity is counteracted by the fire atoms which force the water atoms to combine to form crystals. Instrumental fluidity is at the basis of solids melting upon contact with fire. This contact causes the bonds that made the atoms from the structure associated with the solid to get broken.

Proposition 5.6. Conjunction and disjunction of āpas in the cloud causes electricity to flow. (VS 5.2.11)

Proposition 5.7. The motion of the hand is explained by the action of the mind. (VS 5.2.14)

Proposition 5.8. Space, time, and ākāśa are not associated with motion and are thus non-dynamic. (VS 5.2.21)

This is because, as previously mentioned, space, time, and ākāśa are non-atomic. The coinherence of non-dynamic entities is excluded from action. (VS 5.2.23)

Proposition 5.9. Space is described by qualities. (VS 5.2.25)

Since space is not associated by with motion, it can only be associated with qualities such as location.

Proposition 5.10. Time is defined by way of causality. (VS 5.2.26)

Impressions

Proposition 6.1. Non-reality is from non-existence. (VS 6.2.9)

Proposition 6.2. From association arise impressions. (VS 6.2.10-11)

Universal and transforming qualities

Proposition 7.1. Specific properties like form, color, and so on, are transient properties in matter since they characterize a non-eternal substance. (VS 7.1.2)

Proposition 7.2. Qualities are eternal in āpas, tejas, and vāyu, since these substances are eternal. (VS 7.1.4)

The atoms are ordinarily indestructible and to that extent their properties are well-defined. But in creation and dissolution, the atoms do transform amongst each other and into energy.

Proposition 7.3. The recognition and non-recognition of the atom's extension is explained in eternals. (VS 7.1.8)

In consequence of extension, fullness is produced. The fullness of extension seems to correspond to a wave.

Proposition 7.4. The opposite of fullness is the atom. (VS 7.1.10)

This then sets up the duality of singularity and plurality. By these comparisons large and small are described. (VS 7.1.17)

Proposition 7.5. The roundness of the atom is universal. (VS 7.1.20)

Even though the atom cannot be perceived through the senses, it has to be the same from any direction or it must necessarily possess symmetry. In the conventional two or three dimension visualization that we are used to, it is a circle or a spherical shape.

Proposition 7.6. Ākāśa and consciousness, by virtue of their expansiveness, are pervasive. (VS 7.1.22)

Proposition 7.7. In consequence of the absence of extension, the mind is small. (VS 7.1.23)

Proposition 7.8. Form, touch, taste and odor in their multiplicity indicate the existence of wholeness. 7.2.1.

Likewise separateness is distinct. (VS 7.2.2)

Proposition 7.9. There is neither conjunction nor disjunction in cause and effect since neither exists independently. (VS 7.2.13)

According to Praśastapāda, universals are of two kinds: higher and lower. A universal pervades its instances and occurs in the same form in many things, and is the source of our ideas of class inclusion, since it inheres in all its loci simultaneously.

Consciousness and mind

Proposition 8.1. Ātman and manas are not to be seen in substances. (VS 8.1.2)

Light has outer and inner aspects. The outer light is generated by atoms of tejas while the inner light is a consequence of consciousness. The intuition associated with the inner light is called *jyotiṣa*. The two lights are taken to be connected. The yoga books speak of three skies which are the physical sky (*bhautika ākāśa* or *bhūtākāśa*), the sky of the mind (*citta ākāśa*), and the sky of consciousness (*cid ākāśa*). Of these, the sky of consciousness is the most subtle and powerful and it is this that engenders the connections with the other two skies. The sky of the mind is not fully illumined and its darkness that causes the individual to think that the physical sky is the primary reality.

Proposition 8.2. The cognition of the universal and the particular is in substances with attribute and motion. (VS 8.1.6)

Proposition 8.3. Cognitions arising in different substances are not causes of one another. (VS 8.1.10)

Types of Non-Existence

Proposition 9.1. There is no reality preceding the emergence of physical motion and qualities. (VS 9.1.1)

This implies that what is identifiable is associated with motion.

Proposition 9.2. The ātman is perceived by the senses when there is a particular conjunction of the ātman and mind in the ātman. (VS 9.1.11)

Proposition 9.3. Memory arises from the conjunction of consciousness with the mind and the stored impressions. (VS 9.2.6)

Proposition 9.3 provides the mechanism for the influence of consciousness (ātman) on physical processes. The conjunction of the ātman and mind is not in the physical plane and, therefore, it does not affect the material world.

THE VAIŚEṢIKA SŪTRA OF KAṆĀDA

Chapter 1

First Āhnika

1. अथातो धर्मं व्याख्यास्यामः ॥१।१।१॥

athāto dharmaṃ vyākhyāsyāmaḥ ॥1.1.1॥

Now, then, we shall explain the dharma. 1.1.1.

The Vaiśeṣika is concerned with explaining the physical universe, and dharma represents the laws of reality.

2. यतोऽभ्युदयनिः श्रेयसिद्धिः स धर्मः ॥१।१।२॥

yato'bhyudayaniḥ śreyasiddhiḥ sa dharmaḥ ॥1.1.2॥

By which enlightenment and understanding is obtained is dharma. 1.1.2.

3. तद्वचनादाम्नायस्य प्रामाण्यम् ॥१।१।३॥

tadvacanādāmnāyasya prāmāṇyam ॥1.1.3॥

Those words [are by] the tradition attested. 1.1.3.

The Padārthas

4. धर्मविशेषप्रसूताद्द्रव्यगुणकर्मसामान्यविशेषसमवायानां पदार्थानां साधर्म्यवैधर्म्याभ्यां तत्वज्ञानान्निःश्रेयसम् ॥१।१।४॥

dharmaviśeṣaprasūtāddravyaguṇakarmasāmānyaviśeṣasama vāyānāṃ padārthānāṃ sādharmyavaidharmyābhyāṃ tattvajñānānniḥśreyasam ॥1.1.4॥

Born of the nature of the law, dravya (substance), guṇa (qualities), karman (motion), sāmānya (universality), viśeṣa (particularity), samavāya (inherence) of the padārthas and [the interplay between] similar and dissimilar characteristics comes true knowledge that leads to enlightenment. 1.1.4.

This describes the six ontological categories of reality which shall be represented by the letters *d,g,k,u,v,s* (notice *u* represents sāmānya whereas *s* represents samavāya) that constitute a fundamental sextuple. Three of these, dravya (substance), guṇa (qualities), karman (motion) represent things and their properties and these are the components of standard physics that builds on elementary particles, their physical characteristics, and their mutual interactions. The motion may be of many types including linear and rotational, and the specific kind may be associated with the qualities of the substance.

These three represent physical reality (prakṛti) that may be represented by the triad (*d, g, k*) below in which the substance is shown at the bottom as is customary for prakṛti.

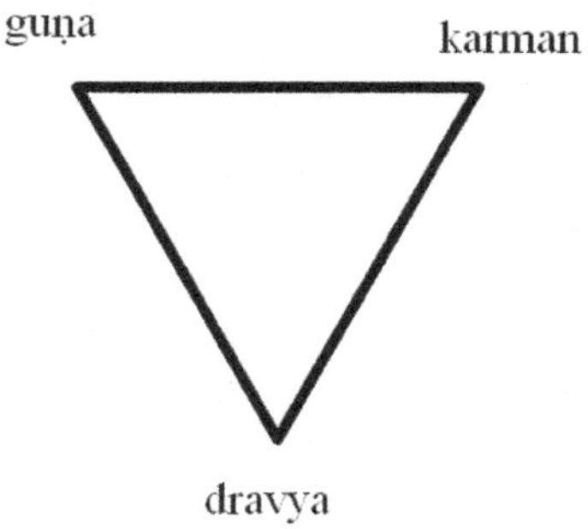

Matter (dravya), qualities (guṇa), and motion (karman)

The ontology of Vaiśeṣika includes three other categories that are associated with perception. The mind has the capacity to distinguish between universal and particular properties, where the latter are the qualia, the subjective experiences of the observer. The meeting point between the physical world and the world of cognition is the category of samavāya which will be discussed further in later chapters. The triad corresponding to perception is given below as the puruṣa triad:

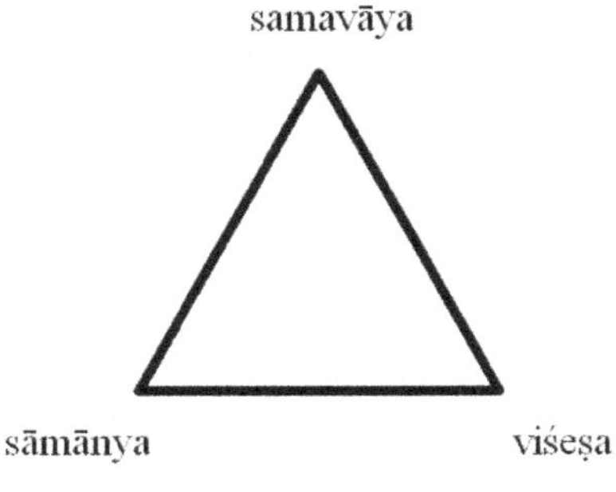

Universal (sāmānya), viśeṣa (particular), and samavāya (inherence)

Taken together, the sextuple (*d,g,k,u,v,s*) may be represented as an intersection of the above two triangles:

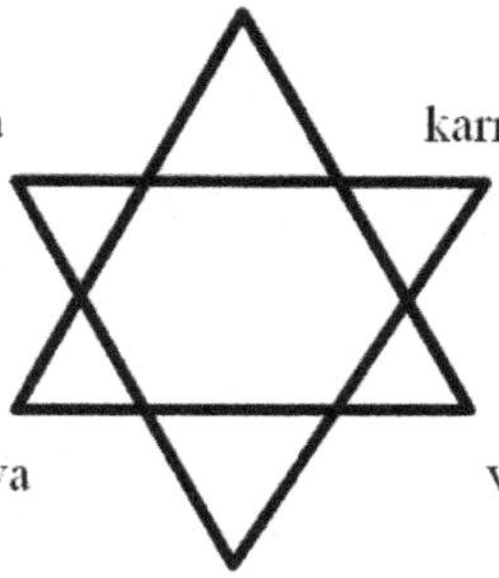

Matter and cognition

As we see this constitutes the familiar yantra that is used for both materiality and consciousness.

Substances and their Qualities

5. पृथिव्यापस्तेजो वायुराकाशं कालो दिगात्मा मन इति द्रव्याणि ॥१।१।५॥

pṛthivyāpastejo vāyurākāśam kālo digātmā mana iti dravyāṇi ॥1.1.5॥

Pṛthivī, āpas, tejas, vāyu, ākāśa, time, space, ātman, and manas are the dravyas. 1.1.5.

As mentioned before, the substances pṛthivī, āpas, tejas, vāyu are respectively solidity, fluidity, light, and gaseousness. Each material is composed of atoms of these four types. Solid matter also contains āpas since it will at high temperature become a liquid.

The dravya ākāśa is ether, the substratum that makes it possible for fields to exist and interactions between substances to be possible. The dravya ātman is consciousness, and manas is the mind.

6. रूपरसगन्धस्पर्शाः संख्याः परिमाणानि पृथक्त्वं संयोगविभागौ परत्वापरत्वे बुद्धयः सुखदुःखे इच्छाद्वेषौ प्रयत्नाश्च गुणाः ॥१।१।६॥

rūparasagandhasparśāḥ saṃkhyāḥ parimāṇāni pṛthaktvam saṃyogavibhāgau paratvāparatve buddhyaḥ sukhaduḥkhe icchādveṣau prayatnāśca guṇāḥ ॥1.1.6॥

Form, taste, odor, touch, number, measures, separateness, conjunction, disjunction, otherness, sameness, intelligence, desire, aversion, effort, and so on, are the qualities. 1.1.6.

The measures for atoms include mass and size; other qualities are a consequence of internal motions of the atoms or the gross motion of the substance under consideration and the relationship (such as separateness, conjunction, and disjunction) with other substances. Even though some of the relationships between substances are in themselves a matter of degree in which judgment is involved, these qualities may be termed external.

Further qualities such as intelligence are related to the workings of the mind which, in turn, can have effect on a physical system. Thus the mind's volitional act of moving the arm sets forth the chain of physical processes that leads to the performance of this action.

7. उत्क्षेपणमवक्षेपणमाकुञ्चनं प्रसारणं गमनमिति कर्माणि ॥१।१।७॥

utkṣepaṇamavakṣepaṇamākuñcanaṃ prasāraṇaṃ gamanamiti karmāṇi ॥1.1.7॥

Upward motion, downward motion, pulling, pushing and [general] motion are the different kinds of motions. 1.1.7.

These motions include linear and rotational motions and combination of these two motions. It is implicit that the motion is with respect to the observer.

8. सदनित्यं द्रव्यवत्कार्यं कारणं सामान्यविशेषवदिति द्रव्यगुणकर्मणामविशेषः ॥१।१।८॥

sadanityaṃ dravyavatkāryaṃ kāraṇaṃ sāmānyaviśeṣavaditi dravyaguṇakarmaṇāmaviśeṣaḥ ॥1.1.8॥

Potential, transitoriness, substance-carried effort, cause, universality and particularity are grounded on dravya, guṇa, and karman. 1.1.8.

This indicates that the outer categories of substance, quality and motion provide the basis for their interpretation for the cognitive categories related to universality, particularity, and inherence.

9. द्रव्यगुणयोः सजातीयारम्भकत्वं साधर्म्यं ॥१।१।९॥

dravyaguṇayoḥ sajātīyārambhakatvaṃ sādharmyaṃ ॥1.1.9॥

The [categories] dravya and qualities generate their own classes as a rule.1.1.9.

The categories do not inter-transform. For example, motion cannot be converted into any of the qualities associated with the substance.

10. द्रव्याणि द्रव्यान्तरमारभन्ते गुणाश्च गुणान्तरम् ॥१।१।१०॥

dravyāṇi dravyāntaramārabhante guṇāśca guṇāntaram ॥1.1.10॥

From dravya other dravyas and from qualities other qualities emerge. 1.1.10.

Within each padārtha, there may be interconversion.

11. कर्म कर्मसाध्यं न विद्यते॥१।१।११॥

karmaṃ karmasādhyaṃ na vidyate ॥1.1.11॥

From motion, [new] motion is not known. 1.1.11.

There is no transformation of motion into another motion.

12. न द्रव्यं कार्यं कारणञ्च बधति ॥१।१।१२॥

na dravyaṃ kāryaṃ kāraṇañca badhati ॥1.1.12॥

Dravya, motion and the cause are not [mutually] destructive. 1.1.12.

This indicates the disjunction between the classes of the substance, the cause, and the motion associated with the substance.

13. उभयथा गुणाः ॥१।१।१३॥

ubhayathā guṇāḥ ॥1.1.13॥

By both [motion and cause] qualities [may be destroyed]. 1.1.13.

Thus motion may transform the rest-state qualities associated with the object.

14. कार्य्यविरोधि कर्म ॥१।१।१४॥

kāryyavirodhi karma ॥1.1.14॥

Action (kārya) is opposed by reaction (karman). 1.1.14.

If a stone is pressed with a finger, the finger is in turn pressed by the stone. If a horse draws a stone tied to a rope, it will be equally drawn back by the stone.

15. क्रियागुणवत् समवायिकारणमिति द्रव्यलक्षणम् ॥१।१।१५॥

kriyāguṇavat samavāyikāraṇamiti dravyalakṣaṇam ॥1.1.15॥

Motion and qualities and causal inherence are the characteristics of dravya. 1.1.15.

In other words, the definition of the dravya is on the basis of qualities that are obtained by cognitive inherence.

16. द्रव्याश्रय्यगुणवान् संयोगविभागेष्वकारणमनपेक्ष इति गुणलक्षणम् ॥१।१।१६॥

dravyāśrayyaguṇavān saṃyogavibhāgeṣvakāraṇamanapekṣa iti guṇalakṣaṇam ॥1.1.16॥

Grounded in dravya, devoid of quality for itself, not causative of conjunction or disjunction are the signs of a guṇa (attribute). 1.1.16.

The qualities are objective although they are impressed on the mind. Qualities do not possess other qualities which avoids the problem of logical infinite recursion.

17. एकद्रव्यमगुणं संयोगविभागेष्वनपेक्षकारणमिति कर्मलक्षणम्॥१।१।१७॥

Ekadravyamaguṇaṃ saṃyogavibhāgeṣvanapekṣakāraṇamiti karmalakṣaṇam ॥1.1.17॥

Residing in one dravya, devoid of qualities, and not causative of conjunction or disjunction are the qualities of motion.1.1.17.

Motion may be of different type, but it does not have qualities.

18. द्रव्यगुणकर्मणां द्रव्यं कारणं सामान्यम् ॥१।१।१८॥

dravyaguṇakarmaṇāṃ dravyaṃ kāraṇaṃ sāmānyam ॥1.1.18॥

In dravyas, qualities, and motion, dravya is the universal cause. 1.1.18.

Dravya is the ground on which qualities and motions are defined. Thus inherence (samavāya) may only be associated with dravya.

19. तथा गुणाः ॥१।१।१९॥

tathā guṇāḥ ॥1.1.19॥

Likewise [is true of] qualities. 1.1.19.

20. संयोगविभागवेगानां कर्म समानम् ॥१।१।२०॥

saṃyogavibhāgavegānāṃ karma samānam ॥1.1.20॥

Conjunctions, disjunctions and momentum are equivalent to motion.1.1.20.

These represent different aspects of motion as defined with respect to different observers.

21. न द्रव्याणां कर्म ॥१।१।२१॥

na dravyāṇāṃ karma ॥1.1.21॥

Motion is not [the cause of] dravyas. 1.1.21.

This is the reason motion is defined as a separate ontological category.

22. व्यतिरेकात् ॥१।१।२२॥

vyatirekāt ॥1.1.22॥

[On account of] exclusion. 1.1.22.

Motion is independent of the dravya for it is exhausted in the chain of action and reaction.

23. द्रव्याणां द्रव्यं कार्यं सामान्यम् ॥१।१।२३॥

dravyāṇāṃ dravyaṃ kāryaṃ sāmānyam ॥1.1.23॥

Of many dravyas, one dravya and one effect are common. 1.1.23.

This explains why the effect of many substances may be added up, implying that the effect of many dravyas can be equivalent to that of one. In other words, there is an additive property associated with dravyas.

24. गुणवैधर्म्यान्न कर्मणां कर्म ॥१।१।२४॥

guṇavaidharmyānna karmaṇāṃ karma ॥1.1.24॥

Due to difference in qualities, many motions do not lead to one motion. 1.1.24.

This is most clearly seen in examining the simultaneous workings of outer and intrinsic motions that are not additive. As another example, rotational motion cannot be transformed to linear motion.

25. द्वित्वप्रभृतयः संख्याः पृथक्त्वसंयोगविभागाश्च ॥१।१।२५॥

dvitvaprabhṛtayaḥ saṃkhyāḥ pṛthaktvasaṃyogavibhāgāśca ॥1.1.25॥

Twoness, discreteness and numerousness, separateness, conjunction, disjunction [are generated by many dravyas and not just one]. 1.1.25.

Properties related to location and motion are shared by many dravyas.

26. असमवायात् सामान्यकार्यं कर्म न विद्यते ॥१।१।२६॥

asamavāyāt sāmānyakāryaṃ karma na vidyate ॥1.1.26॥

Lacking inherence [in a single dravya], universal action is not understood to be one [class of] motion. 1.1.26.

Motion is correctly defined only in relative terms.

27. संयोगानां द्रव्यम् ॥१।१।२७॥

saṃyogānāṃ dravyam ॥1.1.27॥

[The one action in the] dravya is from several conjunctions. 1.1.27.

The conjunctions are additive. Thus many impressed forces may be replaced by a single equivalent force.

28. रूपाणां रूपम् ॥१।१।२८॥

rūpāṇāṃ rūpam ॥1.1.28॥

By many forms one form. 1.1.28.

Likewise guṇas are additive. Thus the quality of measure (mass) is additive as in the sum of mass or other qualities like electric charge.

29. गुरूत्वप्रयत्नसंयोगानामुत्क्षेपणम् ॥१।१।२९॥

gurutvaprayatnasaṃyogānāmutkṣepaṇam ॥1.1.29॥

Gravitation and effort in conjunction result in upward motion. 1.1.29.

This explains how a piece of stone thrown up first flies up and then comes back to hit the ground.

30. संयोगविभागाश्च कर्मणाम् ॥१।१।३०॥

saṃyogavibhāgāśca karmaṇāṃ ॥1.1.30॥

Conjunctions and disjunctions are associated with [objects in] motion. 1.1.30.

This indicates that motion is fundamental to properties that inhere and are consequently cognized.

31. कारणसामान्ये द्रव्यकर्मणां कर्माकारणमुक्तम्॥१।१।३१॥

kāraṇasāmānye dravyakarmaṇāṃ karmākāraṇamuktam ॥1.1.31॥

[Amongst] causes related to karman and dravya, karman is said not to be the cause. 1.1.31.

The basic causes are thus related to dravya and not motion.

Second Āhnika

The Universal and the Particular

1. कारणाभावात्कार्याभावः ॥१।२।१॥

kāraṇābhāvātkāryābhāvaḥ ॥1.2.1॥

In absence of cause, [there is] absence of effect (motion).1.2.1.

The object remains in its state of rest or motion in the absence of cause.

2. न तु कार्याभावात् कारणाभावः॥१।२।२॥

na tu kāryābhāvāt kāraṇābhāvaḥ ॥1.2.2॥

From absence of motion no absence of cause [may be inferred]. 1.2.2.

The converse is not true since several applied causes (forces) may merely cancel each other out so that there is no resultant motion.

3. सामान्यं विशेष इति बुद्ध्यपेक्षम् ॥१।२।३॥

sāmānyaṃ viśeṣa iti buddhyapekṣam ॥1.2.3॥

The [properties of] universal and particular are ascertained by the mind. 1.2.3.

The interactions of the objects can only be local and, therefore, the properties of the collective that are associated with the universal and the particular may only be associated with the mind.

4. भावोऽनुवृत्तेरेव हेतुत्वात् सामान्यम् ॥१।२।४॥

bhāvao'nuvṛttereva hetutvāt sāmānyam ॥1.2.4॥

Reality is the intermittent cause of recurrence and hence a universal.1 2.4.

The idea of reality cannot be explained in terms of local interactions and it is thus universal.

5. द्रव्यत्वं गुणत्वं कर्मत्वञ्च सामान्यानि विशेषञ्च ॥१।२।५॥

dravyatvaṃ guṇatvaṃ karmatvañca sāmānyani viśeṣañca ॥1.2.5॥

Dravyatva, guṇatva and karmatva are both universal and particular.1.2.5.

They are universal in the sense of the categories they define and particular in the specifics they convey.

6. अन्यत्रान्त्येभ्यो विशेषेभ्यः ॥१।२।६॥

anyatrāntyebhyo viśeṣebhyaḥ ॥1.2.6॥

Leaving aside the particularity that remains. 1.2.6.

This addresses the paradox in the classification of the universal and the particular. The universal categories (padārthas) in themselves constitute a particularity. This is the fundamental paradox associated with a general statement that is given a truth value (commonly known as the liar paradox). Many centuries after Kaṇāda, Bhartṛhari addresses this directly in his consideration of the truth value of the statement *sarvam mithyā bravīmi* "everything I am saying is false".

On Sattā

7. सदिति यतोद्रव्यगुणकर्मसु सा सत्ता ॥१।२।७॥

saditi yatodravyaguṇakarmasu sā sattā ॥1.2.7॥

Existence is [self-defined]. [Thus] dravya, guṇa and karman are sattā (potential). 1.2.7.

This defines the outer reality collective of substance, qualities, and motion as a potential.

8. द्रव्यगुणकर्मभ्योऽर्थान्तरं सत्ता ॥१।२।८॥

dravyaguṇakarmabhyo'rthāntaraṃ sattā ॥1.2.8॥

The class sattā is different [from] dravya, guṇa and karman. 1.2.8.

The class sattā cannot be the same as that of the constituent classes of substance, qualities, and motion.

9. गुणकर्मसु च भावान्न कर्म न गुणः ॥१।२।९॥

guṇakarmasu ca bhāvānna karma na guṇaḥ ॥1.2.9॥

Existing in guṇa and karman (padārtha), it is not guṇa or karman.1.2.9.

This acknowledges the subtle distinction that exists between classes and class of classes.

10. सामान्यविशेषाभावेन च॥१।२।१०॥

sāmānyaviśeṣābhāvena ca ॥1.2.10॥

And also due to the absence of the universal and specific. 1.2.10.

A padārtha is supposed to be qualified by the properties of the universal and the particular but the class sattā cannot be so qualified.

11. अनेकद्रव्यवत्त्वेन द्रव्यत्वमुक्तम् ॥१।२।११॥

anekadravyavattvena dravyatvamuktam ॥1.2.11॥

The class of dravyatva results when many dravyas inhere. 1.2.11.

The class of dravyatva is the inherence of many different dravyas.

12. सामान्यविशेषाभावेन च॥१।२।१२॥

sāmānyaviśeṣābhāvena ca ॥1.2.12॥

And also due to the absence of the universal and the particular. 1.2.12.

Such a class also cannot have the distinction between the universal and the particular.

13. तथा गुणेषुभावाद्गुणत्वमुक्तम् ॥१।२।१३॥

tathā guṇeṣubhāvādguṇatvamuktam ॥1.2.13॥

Likewise it is said of the class of qualities.1.2.13.

14. सामान्यविशेषाभावेन च॥१।२।१४॥

sāmānyaviśeṣābhāvena ca ॥1.2.14॥

And also due to the absence of universality and particularity. 1.2.14.

15. कर्मसु भावात् कर्मत्वमुक्तम् ॥१।२।१५॥

karmasu bhāvāt karmatvamuktam ॥1.2.15॥

By being in motion, the class of motions is defined.1.2.15.

16. सामान्यविशेषाभावेन च ॥१।२।१६॥

sāmānyaviśeṣābhāvena ca ॥1.2.16॥

And also due to the absence of universality and particularity. 1.2.16.

17. सदितिलिङ्गाविशेषाद् विशेषलिङ्गाभावाच्चैको भावः ॥१।२।१७॥

saditiliṅgāviśeṣād viśeṣaliṅgābhāvācchaiko bhāvaḥ ॥1.2.17॥

The real [or potential], defined due to the absence of particularity and also lack of specific qualities, is just one thing.1.2.17.

This explains the uniqueness of reality.

CHAPTER 2

First Āhnika

Properties of the Dravyas

1. रूपरसगन्धस्पर्शवती पृथिवी ॥२।१।१॥

rūparasagandhasparśavatī pṛthivī ॥2.1.1॥

Form, taste, odor, and touch [are the qualities of] pṛthivī. 2.1.1.

We are now speaking of basic atoms of different kind. Pṛthivī has mass and size and it represents the principal mass of a substance. According to Śaṅkara Miśra, form and touch derive from energy alone, whereas taste and smell are related to mass.

2. रूपरसस्पर्शवत्य आपो द्रवाः स्निग्धाः ॥२।१।२॥

rūparasasparśavatya āpo dravāḥ snigdhāḥ ॥2.1.2॥

Form, taste, touch [are the qualities of] āpas [together with] fluidity and viscidity. 2.1.2.

Āpas has mass and size and it is also associated with fluidity and viscidity. Since any material can enter the fluid state, the āpas atom is smaller than the pṛthivī atom.

3. तेजो रूपस्पर्शवत् ॥२।१।३॥

tejo rūpasparśavat ॥2.1.3॥

Tejas has [the qualities of] form and touch. 2.1.3.

Tejas, which represents light and heat, has no mass. Clearly it corresponds to the idea of the photon.

4. स्पर्शवान् वायुः ॥२।१।४॥

sparśavān vāyuḥ ॥2.1.4॥

Touch [is the quality of] vāyu. 2.1.4.

Vāyu represents the constituent atom that causes matter to break off and be carried away (decay). These four, pṛthivī, āpas, tejas, and vāyu are atomic because they have specific qualities. If touch were to be taken to be local, vāyu will have mass but Śaṅkara Miśra does not think so.

5. त आकाशे न विद्यन्ते ॥२।१।५॥

ta ākāśe na vidyante ॥2.1.5॥

These [aforementioned qualities] in ākāśa are not available. 2.1.5.

Since ākāśa does not have specific qualities that can be measured, it is taken to be non-atomic. It is the ground upon which continuous processes exist.

6. सर्पिर्जतुमधूच्छिष्टानामग्निसंयोगाद् द्रवत्वमद्भिः सामान्यम् ॥२।१।६॥

sarpirjatumadhūcchiṣṭānāmagnisaṃyogād dravatvamadbhiḥ sāmānyam ॥2.1.6॥

Ghee, lac, honey-wax and fire in conjunction [lead to] fluidity universally. 2.1.6.

The melting of organic solids (such as ghee or honey-wax) by fire is well established.

7. त्रपुसीसलोहरजतसुवर्णनामग्निसंयोगाद् द्रवत्वमद्भिः सामान्यम् ॥२।१।७॥

trapusīsaloharajatasuvarṇāmagnisaṃyogād

dravatvamadbhiḥ sāmānyam ॥2.1.7॥

Tin, lead, iron, silver, gold and fire in conjunction [lead to] fluidity universally. 2.1.7.

The fluidity of metals under conditions of high temperature is well known.

8. विषाणि ककुद्वान् प्रान्तेबालधिः सास्नवान् इति गोत्वे दृष्टं लिङ्गम् ॥२।१।८॥

visāṇi kakudvān prāntebāladhiḥ sāsnavān iti gotve dṛṣṭaṃ liṅgam ॥2.1.8॥

Horned, humped, hair-tip tailed, dewlapped are for the cow the observed identifiers. 2.1.8.

Gross bodies (whether elements or complex organisms) are identified by their attributes.

9. स्पर्शश्च वायोः ॥२।१।९॥

sparśaśca vāyoḥ ॥2.1.9॥

And touch is [the identifier of] vāyu. 2.1.9.

To the extent touch is felt as distributed, it is a non-local sense.

10. न च दृष्टानां स्पर्श इत्यदृष्टलिङ्गो वायुः ॥२।१।१०॥

na ca dṛṣṭānāṃ sparśa ityadṛṣṭaliṅgo vāyuḥ ॥2.1.10॥

And not for the visible [dravyas] touch [is the identifier], it is the identifier of vāyu. 2.1.10.

Therefore, touch is not considered visible for the latter is associated with precision.

11. अद्रव्यवत्त्वेन द्रव्यम् ॥२।१।११॥

adravyavattvena dravyam ॥2.1.11॥

By [inherence in] no [other] dravya, [vāyu] is an [independent] dravya. 2.1.11.

Characterized by a distributed property, vāyu is different from other dravyas.

12. क्रियावत्त्वात् गुणवत्त्वाञ्च॥२।१।१२॥

kriyāvattvāt guṇavattvāñca ॥2.1.12॥

[Also] by [virtue of its physical] motion and qualities. 2.1.12.

Naturally, its properties are different from that of other atoms.

13. अद्रव्यत्वेन नित्यत्वमुक्तम् ॥२।१।१३॥

adravyatvena nityatvamuktam ॥2.1.13॥

By [inherence in] no [other] dravya, [vāyu] is said to be eternal. 2.1.13.

It is also different in its property of being eternal.

14. वायोर्वायुसम्मूर्च्छनं नानात्वलिङ्गम् ॥२।१।१४॥

vāyorvāyusammūrcchanaṃ nānātvaliṅgam ॥2.1.14॥

[Since] vāyu and vāyu conjoin, [its] multiplicity is indicated. 2.1.14.

This multiplicity is in accord with its atomic nature.

15. वायुसन्निकर्षे प्रत्यक्षाभावाद् दृष्टं लिङ्गम् न विद्यते ॥२।१।१५॥

vāyusannikarṣe pratyakṣābhāvād dṛṣṭaṃ liṅgam na vidyate ॥2.1.15॥

[In] vāyu's proximity, absent tangibility, a visible sign does not exist. 2.1.15.

Thus vāyu does not interact strongly with other atoms.

16. सामान्यतोदृष्टाञ्चाविशेषः ॥२।१।१६॥

sāmānyatodṛṣṭāñcāviśeṣaḥ ॥2.1.16॥

[And by the rule of] general visibility, no particularity [inheres in vāyu]. 2.1.16.

Vāyu, therefore, acts like a field.

17. तस्मादागमिकम् ॥२।१।१७॥

tasmādāgamikam ॥2.1.17॥

This [agrees with] tradition. 2.1.17.

This is in accord also with the intuition about subtle wind.

18. संज्ञा कर्म्म त्वस्मद्विशिष्टानां लिङ्गम् ॥२।१।१८॥

saṃjñā karmma tvasmadviśiṣṭānāṃ liṅgam ॥2.1.18॥

Naming and agency are sentient [agents'] identifiers. 2.1.18.

Agency implies apartness and this leads to naming and action.

19. प्रत्यक्षप्रवृत्तत्वात् संज्ञाकर्म्मणः ॥२।१।१९॥

pratyakṣapravṛttatvāt saṃjñākarmmaṇaḥ ॥2.1.19॥

Observation-centering [leads to] naming and actions. 2.1.19.

The capacity to observe is the first step to action.

20. निष्क्रमणं प्रवेशनमित्याकाशस्य लिङ्गम् ॥२।१।२०॥

niṣkramaṇaṃ praveśanamityākāśasya liṅgam ॥2.1.20॥

Egress and ingress are ākāśa's identifiers. 2.1.20.

The element ākāśa, like space, is characterized by ingress and egress.

21. तदलिङ्गमेकद्रव्यत्वात् कर्म्मणः॥२।१।२१॥

tadaliṅgamekadravyatvāt karmmaṇaḥ ॥2.1.21॥

That [egress and ingress] is not capacitative -- being in one dravya -- of motion. 2.1.21

Therefore ākāśa is not associated with motion.

22. कारणान्तरानुक्लृप्तिवैधर्म्याञ्च ॥२।१।२२॥

kāraṇāntarānuklṛptivaidharmyāñca ॥2.1.22॥

Also because of [ākāśa's] difference in characteristics [with other dravyas]. 2.1.22.

In this lack of motion and non-atomicity, ākāśa is different from other dravyas.

23. संयोगादभावः कर्मणः ॥२।१।२३॥

saṃyogādabhāvaḥ karmaṇaḥ ॥2.1.23॥

In conjunction [there is] non-availability of motion. 2.1.23.

The fact that ākāśa can have conjunction with a substance continuously implies that it is not characterized by motion.

24. कारणगुणपूर्वकः कार्यगुणो दृष्टः ॥२।१।२४॥

kāraṇaguṇapūrvakaḥ kāryaguṇo dṛṣṭaḥ ॥2.1.24॥

The qualities of the precedent cause are seen in the qualities of the resultant. 2.1.24.

The previous three sūtras list reasons why ākāśa cannot be one of the other dravyas. Śaṅkara Miśra explains that the resultant guṇas arise from the atomic properties of the constituents and the quality of śabda is not to be found in the other dravyas.

25. कार्यान्तराप्रादुर्भावाच्च शब्दः स्पर्शवतामगुणः ॥२।१।२५॥

kāryāntarāprādurbhāvācca śabdah sparśavatāmaguṇaḥ ॥2.1.25॥

The non-appearance of (similar) other effects [implies that] śabda is not touch-attributed [in other dravyas]. 2.1.25.

Kaṇāda asserts śabda as not associated with other elements for it does not have the property of touch.

26. परत्र समवायात् प्रत्यक्षत्वाञ्च नात्मगुणो न मनोगुणः ॥२।१।२६॥

paratra samavāyāt pratyakṣatvāñca nātmaguṇo na manoguṇaḥ ॥2.1.26॥

[Being] elsewhere inhered, [śabda] perception it is neither an attribute of ātman nor manas. 2.1.26.

Neither is śabda associated with ātman or manas.

27. परिशेषाल्लिङ्गमाकाशस्य ॥२।१।२७॥

pariśeṣāliṅgamākāśasya ॥2.1.27॥

[By the method of exhaustion], śabda is the identifier of ākāśa. 2.1.27.

Thus by eliminating all other possible solutions, it is concluded that śabda is associated with ākāśa.

28. द्रव्यत्त्वनित्यत्वे वायुना व्याख्याते ॥२।१।२८॥

dravyattvanityatve vāyunā vyākhyāte ॥2.1.28॥

Substanceness and eternality [of ākāśa] is explained [as for] vāyu. 2.1.28.

Since it doesn't have localized characteristics, it is eternal like vāyu.

29. तत्त्वम्भावेन ॥२।१।२९॥

tattvambhāvena ॥2.1.29॥

The unity [of ākāśa] exists [in potential or sattā]. 2.1.29.

One can speak of ākāśa not as a localized substance (for it is not atomic) but rather like a field.

30. शब्दलिङ्गाविशेषाद्विशेषलिङ्गाभावाच्च ॥२।१।३०॥

śabdaliṅgāviśesādviśeṣaliṅgābhāvācca ॥2.1.30॥

[Although] śabda-identifiers are lacking and the absence of any [other] particular identifier. 2.1.30.

This adds to the arguments in justification the oneness of ākāśa.

31. तदनुविधानादेकपृथक्त्वञ्चेति ॥२।१।३१॥

tadanuvidhānādekapṛthaktvañceti ॥2.1.31॥

That oneness regime [leads to the quality] of homogeneity. 2.1.31.

The element ākāśa complements the other four elements in its continuous field-like nature as against their atomicity.

Second Āhnika

Further Properties of the Dravyas

1. पुष्पवस्त्रयोः सति सन्निकर्षे गुणान्तराप्रादुर्भावो वस्त्रे गन्धाभावलिङ्गम् ॥२।२।१॥

puṣpavastrayoḥ sati sannikarṣe guṇāntarāprādurbhāvo vastre gandhābhāvaliṅgām ॥2.2.1॥

Flower and cloth together lead to the scent arising in the cloth, even though the cloth does not possess the quality of scent. 2.2.1.

The cloth will smell different in association with a different flower because it doesn't possess the quality of odor.

2. व्यस्थितः पृथिव्यां गन्धः ॥२।२।२॥

vyavasthitaḥ pṛthivyām gandhaḥ ॥2.2.2॥

Established in pṛthivī is smell. 2.2.2.

Smell is used as a marker for mass. Presumably, the intuition used by Kaṇāda was that some molecules of the substance find their way into the nose and are thus recognized.

3. एतेनोष्णता व्याख्याता ॥२।२।३॥

etenoṣṇatā vyākhyātā ॥2.2.3॥

By this heat is explained. 2.2.3.

The smell of the pṛthivī is catalyzed by the heat of the tejas dravya. This indicates that tejas breaks bonds which causes the substance to break free and float away.

4. तेजस उष्णता ॥२।२।४॥

tejasa uṣṇatā ॥2.2.4॥

In tejas is heat. 2.2.4.

It is recognized that tejas is not only light but also heat.

5. अप्सु शीतता ॥२।२।५॥

apsu śītatā ॥2.2.5॥

In liquidity is coldness. 2.2.5.

Liquidity is viewed as a phase from which heat has been taken away. Thus tejas makes for a transition between liquid and vapor.

6. अपरस्मिन्नपरं युगपत् चिरं क्षिप्रमिति काललिङ्गानि ॥२।२।६॥

aparasminnaparaṃ yugapat chiraṃ kṣipramiti kālaliṅgāni ॥2.2.6॥

Closeness, nearness, farness, simultaneity, delay, quickness, all are time-identifiers. 2.2.6.

The passage of time is marked by a variety of terms that are listed.

7. द्रव्यत्वनित्यत्वे वायुना व्याख्याते ॥२।२।७॥

dravyatvanityatve vāyunā vyākhyāte ॥2.2.7॥

Its substantiveness and eternality are explained [as for] vāyu. 2.2.7.

Since time is distributed, it has some properties, such as eternality, that are similar to that of vāyu.

8. तत्त्वम्भावेन ॥२।२।८॥

tattvambhāvena ॥2.2.8॥

The unity [of time] is from [the nature of] reality. 2.2.8.

The unity of time is implicit in our understanding of reality.

9. नित्येष्वभावादनित्येषु भावात्कारणे कालाख्येति ॥२।२।९॥

nityeṣvabhāvādanityeṣu bhāvātkāraṇe kālākhyeti ॥2.2.9॥

In the eternals non-existing and in the non-eternals existing is why time it is so called. 2.2.9.

This sums up beautifully the counterintuitive passage of time when related to eternality. Since time marks change, it cannot exist for an eternal substance, indicating a relativity of time.

10. इत इदमिति यतस्तद्दिश्यं लिङ्गम् ॥२।२।१०॥

ita idamiti yatastaddiśyaṃ liṅgam ॥2.2.10॥

That which gives [usage] as "this [is far away] from this" [is] space identifier. 2.2.10.

Space is defined relatively. Since the question of how far a place is depends on how fast signals go, it means that the definition of space is tied up with the definition of time.

11. द्रव्यत्वनित्यत्वे वायुना व्याख्याते ॥२।२।११॥

dravyatvanityatve vāyunā vyākhyāte ॥2.2.11॥

Its substantiveness and eternality are explained [as for] vāyu. 2.1.11.

Space is distributed and so it must be eternal.

12. तत्त्वम्भावेन ॥२।२।१२॥

tattvambhāvena ॥2.2.12॥

The unity [of space] is in existence. 2.2.12.

Space is a fundamental intuition regarding reality.

13. कार्यविशेषेण नानात्वम्॥२।२।१३॥

kāryaviśeṣeṇa nānātvam ॥2.2.13॥

Motion diversity results in multiplicity [of things]. 2.2.13.

All we see is a consequence of different kinds of motion by different kinds of substances, either by itself or as a consequence of interaction and transformation.

14. आदित्यसंयोगाद्भूतपूर्वाद्भविष्यतो भूताच्च प्राची ॥२।२।१४॥

ādityasaṃyogādbhūtapūrvādbhaviṣyato bhūtācca prācī ॥2.2.14॥

Sun-conjunctions lead to the [divisions of] past, future, that which results from the past (the present), and the east. 2.2.14.

The conventions regarding passage of time arise out of reference to the movement of the sun. This also fixes the east direction.

15. तथा दक्षिण प्रतीची उदीचि च ॥२।२।१५॥

tathā dakṣiṇa pratīcī udīci ca ॥2.2.15॥

And the south, the west and the north. 2.2.15.

The other directions are likewise determined. But as the earth is round, the question of absolute directions is complicated.

16. एतेन दिगन्तरालानि व्याख्यातानि ॥२।२।१६॥

etena digantarālāni vyākhyātāni ॥2.2.16॥

By these the sub-directions are explained. 2.2.16.

In any given frame the directions can be clearly marked.

17. सामान्यप्रत्यक्षाद्विशेषाप्रत्यक्षाद्विशेषस्मृतेश्च संशयः ॥२।२।१७॥

sāmānyapratyakṣādviśeṣāpratyakṣādviśeṣasmṛteśca saṃśayaḥ ॥2.2.17॥

Doubt arises from common sights, particularities that are non-visible, and from particular memories. 2.2.17.

The process of observation is riddled with problems since not all processes are observable to the naked eye. Not all atoms have the same properties, therefore observations may be associated with doubt. The problem with memories arises for what is recorded is not entirely what had transpired.

18. दृष्टटञ्च दृष्टवत् ॥२।२।१८॥

dṛṣṭaṭañca dṛṣṭavat ॥2.2.18॥

From what is seen and what has been seen [also doubt arises]. 2.2.18.

Observations may also vary with time.

19. यथादृष्टमयथादृष्टत्वाच्च ॥२।२।१९॥

yathādṛṣṭamayathādṛṣṭatvācca ॥2.2.19॥

From what is seen is different from what was seen [also doubt arises]. 2.2.19.

These sutras argue that what is seen can appear different to different observers as well as show the limitations of narrative.

20. विद्याऽविद्यातश्च संशयः ॥२।२।२०॥

vidyā'vidyātaśca saṃśayaḥ ॥2.2.20॥

From true and false knowledge [also] doubt arises. 2.2.20.

The questions about doubt lead to the one on what is knowledge.

Nature of Śabda

21. श्रोत्रग्रहणो योऽर्थः स शब्दः ॥२।२।२१॥

śrotragrahaṇo yo'rthaḥ sa śabdaḥ ॥2.2.21॥

[What is] perceived by the ear is śabda. 2.2.21.

The common sound is śabda.

22. तुल्यजातीयेष्वर्थान्तरभूतेषु विशेषस्य उभयथा दृष्टत्वात् ॥२।२।२२॥

tulyajātīyeṣvarthāntarabhūteṣu viśeṣasya ubhayathā dṛṣṭatvāt ॥2.2.22॥

[The properties of śabda in] same-class [dravyas] and in particular substances being different [also leads to doubt]. 2.2.22.

But śabda is more than just ordinary sound.

23. एकद्रव्यत्वान्न द्रव्यम् ॥२।२।२३॥

ekadravyatvānna dravyam ॥2.2.23॥

[As seen in] one dravya [ākāśa], [śabda] is not a dravya. 2.2.23.

It is not a substance for it is associated with other substances.

24. नापि कर्माऽचाक्षुषत्वात् ॥२।२।२४॥

nāpi karmā'cākṣuṣatvāt ॥2.2.24॥

Not also [is it] motion, [for śabda is] invisible. 2.2.24.

Śabda is not a motion for that must be associated with an atomic substance and that it is not.

25. गुणस्य सतोऽपवर्गः कर्मभिः साधर्म्यम् ॥२।२।२५॥

guṇasya sato'pavargaḥ karmabhiḥ sādharmyam ॥2.2.25॥

In guṇa [padārtha], [śabda's] disappearance is similar [in property] to the karman padārtha. 2.2.25.

But it is similar to motion in that it can disappear.

26. सतो लिङ्गाभावात् ॥२।२।२६॥

sato liṅgābhāvāt ॥2.2.26॥

The existence [of śabda is negated] by absence of identifier. 2.2.26.

If it exists in present time, it lacks attributes.

27. नित्यवैधर्म्यात् ॥२।२।२७॥

nityavaidharmyāt ॥2.2.27॥

The eternal is of opposite characteristics [unbounded by time]. 2.2.27.

Thus śabda is not eternal.

28. अनित्यश्चायं कारणतः ॥२।२।२८॥

anityaśrcāyaṃ kāraṇataḥ ॥2.2.28॥

[It is] non-eternal because it [evolves] from a cause. 2.2.28.

It has a beginning and so it must have an end.

29. न चासिद्धं विकारात् ॥२।२।२९॥

na cāsiddhaṃ vikārāt ॥2.2.29॥

Not disproved by modifications. 2.2.29.

Its modification is in intensity or the speed of its passage through different substances.

30. अभिव्यक्तौ दोषात् ॥२।२।३०॥

abhivyaktau doṣāt ॥2.2.30॥

By expression faulted. 2.2.30.

The description of an object need not satisfy the same properties as the object which brings us back to the question of meaning of words.

31. संयोगाद्विभागाच्च शब्दाच्च शब्दनिष्पततिः ॥२।२।३१॥

saṃyogādvibhāgācca śabdācca śabdaniṣpatatiḥ ॥2.2.31॥

By conjunction, disjunction and from [other] sound is śabda produced. 2.2.31.

The production of sound begins with some clear physical event.

32. लिङ्गाच्चानित्यः शब्दः ॥२।२।३२॥

liṅgāccānityaḥ śabdaḥ ॥2.2.32॥

[From] identification also sound is non-eternal. 2.2.32.

Since it can be identified, it has beginning and end and so it cannot be eternal.

33. द्वयोस्तु प्रवृत्तयोरभावात् ॥२।२।३३॥

dvayostu pravṛttayorabhāvāt ॥2.2.33॥

But both also [co-exist] by their nature, from non-existence [of the eternal śabda]. 2.2.33.

In other words, there are two kinds of sound: ordinary one that appears and dies, and eternal sound as śabda.

34. प्रथमाशब्दात् ॥२।२।३४॥

prathamāśabdāt ॥2.2.34॥

From the first śabda. 2.2.34.

The very fact knowledge is possible is due to the eternal śabda.

35. सम्प्रतिपत्तिभावाच्च ॥२।२।३५॥

sampratipattibhāvācca ॥2.2.35॥

From the existence of particular knowledge also. 2.2.35.

The eternality of the subtle śabda is due to the existence of particularity.

36. सन्धिग्धाः सति बहुत्वे ॥२।२।३६॥

sandhigdhāḥ sati bahutve ॥2.2.36॥

Paradox exists due to multiplicity. 2.2.36.

Since the one ātman informs many minds, this numeracy leads to multiple views that may be paradoxical.

37. संख्याभावः सामान्यतः ॥२।२।३७॥

saṃkhyābhāvaḥ sāmānyataḥ ॥2.2.37॥

The potential of count exists in the universal. 2.2.37.

CHAPTER 3

First Āhnika

Existence of the Ātman

1. प्रसिद्धोइन्द्रियार्थाः ॥३॥१।१॥

prasiddhoindriyārthāḥ ॥3.1.1॥

Well established [are the] sensory objects. 3.1.1.

Consciousness is the space in which our sensory experiences lie and our sensory objects are well defined therein.

2. इन्द्रियार्थप्रसिद्धिरिन्द्रियार्थेभ्योऽर्थान्तरस्य हेतुः ॥३॥१।२॥

indriyārthaprasiddhirindriyārthebhyo'rthāntarasya hetuḥ ॥3.1.2॥

Sensory perceptions are of something other than the senses for [knowledge of other objects]. 3.1.2.

Sensory perceptions are not made by the senses but by the self who uses the senses as instruments.

3. सोऽनपदेशः ॥३॥१।३॥

so'napadeśaḥ ॥3.1.3॥

That [equivalence of body as cognizer] is mistaken identity. 3.1.3.

If knowledge is a quality, its perception cannot take place in the body.

4. कारणाज्ञानात् ॥३॥१।४॥

kāraṇājñānāt ॥3.1.4॥

The cause is from false knowledge. 3.1.4.

To take the body as the cognizer of knowledge is error.

5. कार्येषु ज्ञानात् ॥३॥१।५॥

kāryeṣu jñānāt ॥3.1.5॥

In [study of] effects arises knowledge. 3.1.5.

Knowledge arises out of past associations and future expectations.

6. अज्ञानाच्च ॥३॥१।६॥

ajñānācca ॥3.1.6॥

And from false knowledge. 3.1.6.

It also arises out of negation of patterns of expectation that turned out to be incorrect. When we speak in dichotomies, the absence of a thing also leads to knowledge.

Nature of the Proof

7. अन्यदेव हेतुरित्यनपदेशः ॥३॥१।७॥

anyadeva heturityanapadeśaḥ ॥3.1.7॥

The intermittent cause as the other is false identity. 3.1.7.

The causal relationship may be deeper than is indicated superficially.

8. अर्थान्तरं ह्यर्थान्तरस्यानपदेशः ॥३॥१।८॥

arthāntaraṃ hyarthāntarasyānapadeśaḥ ॥3.1.8॥

[Also] another object [as cause] for another object is false identity. 3.1.8.

This means that the context for the proof needs to be clearly enunciated.

9. संयोगि समवाय्येकार्थसमवायि विरोधि च ॥३॥१।९॥

saṃyogi samavāyyekārthasamavāyi virodhi ca ॥3.1.9॥

The conjunct, inherent, one object-inhered, and the contradictory [are all intermittent causes]. 3.1.9.

The setting up of the proof is thus a critical issue.

10. कार्यं कार्य्यान्तरस्य ॥३॥१।१०॥

kāryaṃ kāryyāntarasya ॥3.1.10॥

[Like] motion of something other than physical motion. 3.1.10.

This explains why if A leads to B does not imply the absence of A leads to the absence of B.

11. विरोध्यभूतं भूतस्य ॥३॥१।११॥

virodhyabhūtaṃ bhūtasya ॥3.1.11॥

The non-past is contradicted by the past. 3.1.11.

This and the next two sūtras speak of common errors made in speaking of past and present events.

12. भूतमभूतस्य ॥३॥१।१२॥

bhūtamabhūtasya ॥3.1.12॥

The past [contradicts] the past [that did not happen]. 3.1.12.

13. भूतो भूतस्य ॥३॥१।१३॥

bhūto bhūtasya ॥3.1.13॥

The present [contradicts] the present [that did not happen]. 3.1.13.

14. प्रसिद्धिपूर्वकत्वादपदेशस्य ॥३॥१।१४॥

prasiddhipūrvakatvādapadeśasya ॥3.1.14॥

Validation is preceded by falsification [of some other possibility]. 3.1.14.

This is the most subtle observation that the scientific method is based on the possibility of falsification.

This idea in our times was promoted by the philosopher of science Karl Popper.

15. अप्रसिद्धोऽनपदेशोऽसन् सन्दिग्धश्चानपदेशः ॥३॥१।१५॥

aprasiddho'napadeśo'san sandigdhaśrcānapadeśaḥ ॥3.1.15॥

The non-established and the false lead to paradox and [other] false identities. 3.1.15.

The judgment related to correct understanding is based on the search of possible paradoxes associated with the line of proof.

False Arguments

16. यस्माद्विषाणि तस्मादश्वः ॥३॥१।१६॥

yasmādviṣāṇi tasmādaśvaḥ ॥3.1.16॥

If horned, then a horse. 3.1.16.

Horned = horse is of course false logic.

17. यस्माद्विषाणि तस्मात् गौरिति चानैकान्तिकस्योदाहरणम् ॥३॥१।१७॥

yasmādviṣāṇi tasmāt gauriti cānaikāntikasyodāharaṇam ॥3.1.17॥

If horned, then a cow is also example of multiple identifier. 3.1.17.

There are many horned animals that are not cow. Even a multiplicity of identifiers may not suffice to identify a specific individual.

18. आत्मेन्द्रियार्थसन्निकर्षाध्यन्निष्पध्यते तदन्यत् ॥३॥१।१८॥

ātmendriyārthasannikarṣādhyanniṣpadhyate tadanyat ॥3.1.18॥

[By the] ātman, the senses, and the meaning coming together arises what is the other [knowledge]. 3.1.18.

Knowledge arises out of the ātman and the senses coming together in a space that is different from the one in which the body is located.

19. प्रवृत्तिनिवृत्ति च प्रत्यगात्मनि दृष्टे परत्र लिङ्गम् ॥३॥१।१९॥

pravṛttinivṛtti ca pratyagātmani dṛṣṭe paratra liṅgam ॥3.1.19॥

And the activity and inactivity in every ātman is an identifier when seen elsewhere. 3.1.19.

The identifier is thus in the products of the agency of the specific individual.

Second Āhnika

Mind as Dravya

1. आत्मेन्द्रियार्थसन्निकर्षे ज्ञानस्य भावोऽभावश्च मनसो लिङ्गम् ॥३।२।१॥

ātmendriyārthasannikarṣe jñānasya bhāvo'bhāvaśca manaso liṅgam ॥3.2.1॥

The ātman, the senses, and the meaning coming together, which leads to the presence or absence of a state, become the mind's identifier. 3.2.1.

The mind requires the coming together of the ātman and the senses. This also implies access to the autobiographical memories of the individual.

2. तस्य द्रव्यत्वनित्यत्वे वायुना व्याख्याते ॥३।२।२॥

tasya dravyatvanityatve vāyunā vyākhyāte ॥3.2.2॥

The substanceness and eternality of that are explained by [analogy with] vāyu. 3.2.2.

Since the activity of the mind is distributed, it is somewhat like vāyu, that is atomic and eternal.

3. प्रयत्नयौगपद्याज्ज्ञानायौगपद्याच्चैकम् ॥३।२।३॥

prayatnayaugapadyājjñānāyaugapadyāccaikam ॥3.2.3॥

Volitions being non-simultaneous and knowledge being non-simultaneous indicates one [mind]. 3.2.3.

If there were many minds within the same body then there would be conflict between their activities which is not seen. Different minds would also lead to different judgments and volitions at different times.

Identifiers of the Ātman

4. प्राणापाननिमेषजीवनमनोगतीन्द्रियान्तरविकाराः

सुखदुःखेच्छाद्वेषप्रयत्नाश्चात्मनो लिङ्गानि ॥३।२।४॥

prāṇāpānanimeṣajīvanamagatīndriyāntaravikārāḥ

sukhaduḥkhecchādveṣaprayatnāścātmano liṅgāni ॥3.2.4॥

Prāṇa and apāna (the two breaths), the closing and opening of eye, life, the movement of the mind, hormonal variations of the sensory organs, happiness, sadness, desire, aversion and volition are also the identifiers of the ātman. 3.2.4.

The ātman is identified by subjective experiences and volitional acts.

5. तस्य द्रव्यत्त्वनित्यत्वे वायुना व्याख्याते ॥३।२।५॥

tasya dravyatvanityatve vāyunā vyākhyāte ॥3.2.5॥

The dravyatva and eternality of that are explained by [analogy with] vāyu. 3.2.5.

Since it does not have any qualities and it is distributed, the ātman is eternal and it is a substance.

6. यज्ञदत्त इति सन्निकर्षे प्रत्यक्षाभावात् दृष्टं लिङ्गम् न विद्यते॥३।२।६॥

yajñadatta iti sannikarṣe pratyakṣābhāvāt dṛṣṭam liṅgām na vidyate ||3.2.6||

Yajñadatta's proximity defined clearly is not an identifier [of the ātman]. 3.2.6.

The proximity to his senses of a person named, say, Yajñadatta, is not proof of that person's identity. Likewise, it is not an identifier of the ātman.

7. सामान्यतो दृष्टाच्चाविशेषः ||३|२|७||

sāmānyato dṛṣṭtāccāviśeṣaḥ ||3.2.7||

Universally seen, [the ātman] cannot be inferred in particularity. 3.2.7.

There are no particular properties associated with the ātman.

8. तस्मादागमिकः ||३|२|८||

tasmādāgamikaḥ ||3.2.8||

[It is validated] by the received knowledge. 3.2.8.

We infer that the ātman exists from the very fact that we are capable of generating knowledge.

9. अहमितिशब्दस्य व्यतिरेकान्नागमिकम् ||३|२|९||

ahamitiśabdasya vyatirekānnāgamikam ||3.2.9||

The "I" word's definition is not by [the definition in terms of the body] but by tradition. 3.2.9.

The "I" word emerges from the very meaning associated with it that corresponds to the agency that individuals possess.

10. यदि दृष्टमन्वक्षमहं देवदत्तोहं यज्ञदत्त इति ॥३।२।१०॥

yadi dṛṣṭamanvakṣamahaṃ devadattohaṃ yajñadatta iti ॥3.2.10॥

If perception shows that I am Yajñadatta, [or] I am Devadatta [then there is no doubt]. 3.2.10.

In other words, the self by itself validates the ātman.

11. दृष्ट्यात्मनि लिङ्गे एक एव दृढत्वात् प्रत्यक्षवत् प्रत्ययः ॥३।२।११॥

dṛṣṭyātmani liṅge eka eva dṛḍhatvāta pratyakṣavat pratyayaḥ ॥3.2.11॥

The clear identifiers of the ātman firm up the sense of one and only ātman. 3.2.11.

These identifiers also imply that it is only one.

12. देवदत्तो गच्छति यज्ञदत्तो गच्छतीत्युपचारच्छरीरे प्रत्ययः ॥३।२।१२॥

devadatto gacchati yajñadatto gacchatītyupacāraccharīre pratyayaḥ ॥3.2.12॥

Yajñadatta is going, Devadatta is going, such sense in the body is the cause [of the sense of multiplicity]. 3.2.12.

The idea of multiplicity arises from the many bodies who are informed by the same single ātman.

13. सन्दिग्धस्तूपचारः ॥३।२।१३॥

sandigdhastūpacāraḥ ॥3.2.13॥

The doubt is [which of the body and the self is] primary. 3.2.13.

Does the mind arise out of the body or is the mind primary, is the issue related to the doubts about the ātman.

14. अहमिति प्रत्यगात्मनि भावात् परत्राभावादर्थान्तरप्रत्यक्षः ॥३।२।१४॥

ahamiti pratyagātmani bhāvāt paratrābhāvādarthāntarapratyakṣaḥ ॥3.2.14॥

"I" – the existence [of such an intuition] in one's own ātman and absence in others indicates the perception [of a padārtha] other than the body. 3.2.14.

That one takes oneself to have agency and lack it in others implies a category that is not related to the body.

15. देवदत्तो गच्छतीत्युपचारादभिमानात्तावच्छरीरप्रत्यक्षोऽहङ्कारः ॥३।२।१५॥

devadatto gacchatītyupacārādabhimānāttāvaccharīrapratyakṣo'haṅkārah ||3.2.15||

Devadatta is going and so on, this sense in the body is derivative since the perception from the body is that of the ego. 3.2.15.

The normal understanding is that the body takes its cue from the self.

16. सन्दिग्धस्तूपचारः ||३|२|१६||

sandigdhastūpacārah ||3.2.16||

The doubt is [which of the body and the self is] primary. 3.2.16.

But one can also argue that the body is primary and the self arises in it and this leads to doubt.

17. न तु शरीरविशेषाद् यज्ञदत्तविष्णुमित्रयोर्ज्ञानं विषयः ||३|२|१७||

na tu śarīraviśeṣād yajñadattaviṣṇumitrayorjñānaṃ viṣayah ||3.2.17||

Not from the difference of the bodies is the recognition of [individuals such as] Yajñadatta and Viṣṇumitra determined. 3.2.17.

The knowledge of self is not obtained from the knowledge of the physiology of the body.

18. अहमिति मुख्ययोग्याभ्यां शब्दवद्व्यतिरेकाव्यभिचाराद्विशेषसिद्धेर्नागमिकः ॥३।२।१८॥

ahamiti mukhyayogyābhyām śabdavadvyatirekāvyabhicārādviśeṣasiddhernāgamikaḥ ॥3.2.18॥

"I am" being the primary and visible cognition similar to śabda, whose absence as a rule (in padārthas other than ākāśa) leads to the proof of the particular and not of received knowledge. 3.2.18.

The ego does not lead to universal knowledge.

19. सुखदुःखज्ञाननिष्पत्तयविशेषादैकात्म्यम् ॥३।२।१९॥

sukhaduḥkhajñānaniṣpattayaviśeṣādaikātmyam ॥3.2.19॥

Happiness, sadness, and emergence of knowledge have no particularity which implies one ātman. 3.2.19.

Subjective feelings related to the self are universal. It is this that allows literature to be appreciated within and across cultures.

20. व्यवस्थातो नाना ॥३।२।२०॥

vyavasthāto nānā ॥3.2.20॥

Expressed in multiplicity. 3.2.20.

These feelings are experienced in multiplicity.

21. शास्त्रसामर्थ्याच्च ॥३।२।२१॥

śāstrasāmarthyācca ॥3.2.21॥

And from the proofs of śāstra (science) as well. 3.2.21.

CHAPTER 4

First Āhnika

Eternality

1. सदकारणवन्नित्यम् ॥४।१।१॥

sadakāraṇavannityam ॥4.1.1॥

Existence is uncaused and eternal. 4.1.1.

If existence had a beginning then there must be other existences that existed prior or exist in parallel.

2. तस्य कार्य्यं लिङ्गम्॥४।१।२॥

tasya kāryyaṃ liṅgam ॥4.1.2॥

Its motion (or action) is its identification 4.1.2.

The physical universe is characterized by motions of its constituents.

3. कारणभावात् कार्य्यभावः ॥४।१।३॥

kāraṇabhāvāt kāryyabhāvaḥ ॥4.1.3॥

By being in the cause it follows in the motion. 4.1.3.

The evolution of the universe follows from the nature of the causes that set it in motion.

4. अनित्य इति विशेषतः प्रतिषेधभावः ॥४।१।४॥

anitya iti viśeṣataḥ pratiṣedhabhāvaḥ ॥4.1.4॥

Non-eternality in particularity is forbidden. 4.1.4.

Thus particular qualities are eternal.

5. अविद्या ॥४।१।५॥

avidyā ॥4.1.5॥

[Knowledge of non-eternals alone is] ignorance. 4.1.5.

Thus real knowledge deals with the frame of laws within which the world unfolds.

Perception

6. महत्यनेकद्रव्यवत्तात् रूपा्ञ्चोपलब्धिः ॥४।१।६॥

mahatyanekadravyavattāt rūpāñcopalabdhiḥ ॥4.1.6॥

[A padārtha] with extension is visible from many dravyas in it (as the substratum) and from the attribute form in it. 4.1.6.

Perception requires gross matter which may contain many different dravyas in it.

7. सत्यपि द्रव्यत्तवे महत्तवे रूपसंस्काराभावाद्वायोरनुपलब्धिः ॥४।१।७॥

satyapi dravyattve mahattave rūpāsaṃskārābhāvādvāyoranupalabdhiḥ ॥4.1.7॥

In spite of body and extension, vāyu is invisible owing to the absence of the impression of form. 4.1.7.

In the consideration of collectives, vāyu is ordinarily invisible.

8. अनेकद्रव्यसमवायात् रूपविशेषाच्च रूपोपलब्धिः ॥४।१।८॥

anekadravyasamavāyāt rūpāviśeṣācca rūpopalabdhiḥ ॥4.1.8॥

By the inherence of many dravyas and particularity of the attribute form [the dravya] becomes visible. 4.1.8.

It can become visible (or inferred) by inherence in other dravyas.

9. तेन रसगन्धस्पर्शेषु ज्ञानं व्याख्यातम् ॥४।१।९॥

tena rasagandhasparśeṣu jñānam vyākhyātam ॥4.1.9॥

By this the knowledge in (the qualities of) form, taste, smell and touch are explained. 4.1.9.

According to the Sāṅkhya, the sensory elements also exist in the subtle form (tanmātra) wherein they parallel the five sense organs and the five organs of action.

10. तस्याभावादव्यभिचारः ॥४।१।१०॥

tasyābhāvādavyabhicāraḥ ॥4.1.10॥

[From] its absence no rule is broken. 4.1.10.

Vāyu and tejas do not respond to gravitation.

11. संख्याः परिमाणानि पृथक्त्वं संयोगविभागौ परत्वापरत्वे कर्म च रूपिद्रव्यसमवायात् चाक्षुषाणि ॥४।१।११॥

saṃkhyāḥ parimāṇāni pṛthaktvaṃ saṃyogavibhāgau paratvāparatve karma ca rūpidravyasamavāyāt cākṣuṣāṇi ॥4.1.11॥

Multiplicity (more than one), magnitude, discreteness, conjunction, disjunction, far and near motion too are visible by the inherence of a dravya with visible form. 4.1.11.

The inherence occurs with the corresponding sense organ.

12. अरूपिष्वचाक्षुषाणि॥४।१।१२॥

arūpiṣvacākṣuṣāṇi ॥4.1.12॥

The formless [dravyas] remain invisible 4.1.12.

But their presence may be inferred.

13. एतेन गुणत्वे भावे च सर्वेन्द्रियं व्याख्यातम् ॥४।१।१३॥

etena guṇatve bhāve ca sarvendriyaṃ vyākhyātam ॥4.1.13॥

By this in qualities and in [the category] of reals, all sensory perceptions are explained. 4.1.13.

Second Āhnika

Types of Objects

1. तत् पुनः पृथिव्यादिकार्यद्रव्यं त्रिविधं शरीरेन्द्रियविषयसंज्ञकम् ॥४।२।१॥

tat punaḥ pṛthivyādikāryadravyaṃ trividhaṃ śarīrendriyaviṣayasaṃjñakam ॥4.2.1॥

That again, beginning with pṛthivī, the dravyas with physical motion are in threes as body, senses and quality types. 4.2.1.

This general representation applies both to inanimate and animate objects. In inanimate objects one will speak of object structure, its interactions, and properties, whereas for animate objects one will speak of the body, senses, and qualities.

2. प्रत्यक्षाप्रत्यक्षाणां संयोगस्याप्रत्यक्षत्वात् पञ्चात्मकं न विध्यते ॥४।२।२॥

pratyakṣāpratyakṣāṇāṃ saṃyogasyāpratyakṣatvāt pañcātmakaṃ na vidhyate ॥4.2.2॥

The visible and the non-visible (padārthas) conjoining, a five-element substance does not emerge. 4.2.2.

The five-element substance is composed of all the five elements, but since the vāyu atoms are non-visible, it will not appear overtly.

3. गुणान्तराप्रादुर्भावाच्च न त्रयात्मकम् ॥४।२।३॥

guṇāntarāprādurbhāvācca na trayātmakam ॥4.2.3॥

And in the lacking of attributes not even a three-element [substance emerges]. 4.2.3.

A non-reactive substance appears to be consisting of pṛthivī atoms alone.

4. अणुसंयोगस्त्वप्रतिषिद्धः ॥४।२।४॥

aṇusaṃyogastvapratiṣiddhaḥ ॥4.2.4॥

But conjunction of aṇu is unrestrained. 4.2.4.

The conjunction of the atoms takes place within the dravya.

5. तत्र शरीरं द्विविधं योनिजमयोनिजञ्च ॥४।२।५॥

tatra śarīraṃ dvividhaṃ yonijamayonijañca ॥4.2.5॥

There the body is of two kinds as uterine and non-uterine. 4.2.5.

Śaṅkara Miśra explains that the uterine and the non-uterine refer to embodied and beings of light.

6. अनियतदिग्देशपूर्वकत्वात् ॥४।२।६॥

aniyatadigdeśapūrvakatvāt ॥4.2.6॥

[The non-uterine arise] from an effect with no-specificity in direction and space. 4.2.6.

Now is a statement about classes of conscious beings and Kaṇāda presents his ideas based on symmetry considerations. The uterine ones are beings with bodies and the non-uterine ones are those without physical bodies. Kaṇāda is indicating that there must be conscious structures that are independent of space and time. तस्याभावादव्यभिचारः From its absence no rule is broken. The non-uterine is thus direction independent. The idea here is that the non-uterine beings are more elemental than the uterine ones and they arise out of molecules that are independent of direction.

7. धर्मविशेषाच्च ॥४।२।७॥

dharmaviśeṣācca ॥4.2.7॥

And from particular characteristics of the physical law. 4.2.7.

This is also due to the more basic molecules being non-directional.

8. समाख्याभावाच्च ॥४।२।८॥

samākhyābhāvācca ॥4.2.8॥

And from the reality of identification. 4.2.8.

If consciousness is more fundamental than matter, space, and time, there ought to be conscious beings of diverse kind.

9. संज्ञाया आदित्वात् ॥४।२।९॥

saṃjñāyā āditvāt ॥4.2.9॥

By designation the first ones. 4.2.9.

The first beings are then without bodies.

10. सन्त्ययोनिजाः ॥४।२।१०॥

santyayonijāḥ ॥4.2.10॥

The non-uterine exist. 4.2.10.

The earliest things must not emerge out of directed interactions.

11. वेदलिङ्गाच्च ॥४।२।११॥

vedaliṅgācca ॥4.2.11॥

And from Vedic identification too. 4.2.11.

CHAPTER 5

First Āhnika

Action

1. आत्मसंयोगप्रयत्नाभ्यां हस्ते कर्म ॥५।१।१॥

ātmasaṃyogaprayatnābhyāṃ haste karma ॥5.1.1॥

The ātman's conjunction and volition leads to the hand's motion. 5.1.1.

The movement of the hand can be easily explained in the workings of the muscles. The harder question is the source of the volition that goes behind the movement. If it is claimed that this does not exist and prior processes lead to the supposed volition, then we have no freedom and we are zombies.

2. तथा हस्तसंयोगाच्च मुसले कर्म ॥५।१।२॥

tathā hastasaṃyogācca musle karma ॥5.1.2॥

And hand's conjunction [leads to] pestle's action. 5.1.2.

The volition that sets forth a series of events including the pestle's action is the mystery.

3. अभिघातजे मुसलादौ कर्मणि व्यतिरेकादकारणं हस्तसंयोगः ॥५।१।३॥

abhighātaje muslādau karmaṇi vyatirekādakāraṇam hastasaṃyogaḥ ॥5.1.3॥

[By the] strike [at the mortar], the pestle's [upward] motion is without effort and not by the conjunction of hand. 5.1.3.

The mechanical processes are to be explained by physical law.

4. तथात्मसंयोगो हस्तकर्मणि ॥५।१।४॥

tathātmasaṃyogo hastakarmaṇi ॥5.1.4॥

Such is [not the] ātman's conjunction in the action of the hand. 5.1.4.

But the ātman's role in the volition of the individual cannot be so explained.

5. अभिघातान्मुसलसंयोगाद्धस्ते कर्म ॥५।१।५॥

abhighātānmusalasaṃyogādhaste karma ॥5.1.5॥

From impact and the pestle's conjunction, motion [is produced] in the hand. 5.1.5.

Our actions thus have two components: one that is governed by the laws of physics and the other that is the volition behind the action.

6. आत्मकर्म हस्तसंयोगाच्च ॥५।१।६॥

ātmakarma hastasaṃyogācca ॥5.1.6॥

The ātman's action is in the hand's conjunction also. 5.1.6.

The ātman's action gets cascaded in the events that follow.

7. संयोगाभावे गुरुत्वात् पतनम् ॥५।१।७॥

saṃyogābhāve gurutvāt patanam ॥5.1.7॥

In the absence of conjunction, gravity [causes objects to] fall. 5.1.7.

In the absence of any intervention by a sentient being, gravity causes things to fall.

8. नोदनविशेषाभावान्नोर्ध्वं न तिर्य्यग्गमनम् ॥५।१।८॥

nodanaviśeṣābhāvānnordhvam na tiryyaggamanam ॥5.1.8॥

In the absence of a force, there is no upward motion, sideward motion or motion in general. 5.1.8.

Objects continue to be in their state of rest or motion in the absence of force.

9. प्रयत्नविशेषान्नोदनविशेषः ॥५।१।९॥

prayatnaviśeṣānnodanaviśeṣaḥ ॥5.1.9॥

From a particular effort, a particular force is produced. 5.1.9.

There is a sequence that goes from the initial effort to the force and to a specific motion.

10. नोदनविशेषादुदसनविशेषः ॥५।१।१०॥

nodanaviśeṣādudasanaviśeṣaḥ ॥5.1.10॥

From a particular force, a particular motion is produced. 5.1.10.

11. हस्तकर्मणा दारककर्म व्याख्यातम् ॥५।१।११॥

hastakarmaṇā dārakakarma vyākhyātam ॥5.1.11॥

By the motion of hand, motion in a child is explained. 5.1.11.

12. तथा दग्धस्य विस्फोटने ॥५।१।१२॥

tathā dagdhasya visphoṭane ॥5.1.12॥

Likewise the [lit] fire causing explosion. 5.1.12.

13. यत्नाभावे प्रसुप्तस्य चलनम् ॥५।१।१३॥

yatnābhāve prasuptasya calanam ॥5.1.13॥

In the absence of effort, the sleeping [person's] walking. 5.1.13.

The sleepwalker is not conscious of his movements because the mind has many layers. Many actions of the mind are automatic. This is clear in the Māṇḍūkya Upaniṣad that speaks of the four states of consciousness, namely awake, dreaming, dream sleep, and the turīya (the fourth which is transcendent).

14. तृणे कर्म वायुसंयोगात् ॥५।१।१४॥

tṛṇe karma vāyusaṃyogāt ॥5.1.14॥

In grass, the motion [of leaves] is caused by conjunction with vāyu. 5.1.14.

The swaying of leaves is explained by physical law.

15. मणिगमनम् सूच्यभिसर्पणमदृष्टकारणकम् ॥५।१।१५॥

maṇigamanam sūcyabhisarpaṇamadṛṣṭakāraṇakam ॥5.1.15॥

The movement of the jewel and the approach of the needle, have subtle causes. 5.1.15.

The movement of the compass needle towards the north and the attraction of iron filings to a magnet are due to the subtle force of magnetism.

16. इषावयुगपत्संयोगविशेषाः कर्मान्यत्वे हेतुः ॥५।१।१६॥

iṣāvayugapatsaṃyogaviśeṣāḥ karmānyatve hetuḥ ॥5.1.16॥

In the arrow, successive specific conjunctions explain the successive motions. 5.1.16.

The motion of the arrow may be explained by means of the workings of the potential at successive times.

17. नोदनादाद्यमिषोः कर्म तत्कर्मकारिताच्च संस्कारादुत्तरं तथोत्तरमुत्तरञ्च् ॥५।१।१७॥

nodanādādyamiṣoḥ karma tatkarmakāritācca saṃskārāduttaram tathottaramuttarañc ॥5.1.17॥

The initial pressure [on the bow] leads to the arrow's motion; from that motion is momentum, from which is the motion that follows and the next and so on, similarly. 5.1.17.

The motion can be broken into components.

18. संस्काराभावो गुरुत्वात् पतनम् ॥५।१।१८॥

saṃskārābhāvo gurutvāt patanam ||5.1.18||

In the absence of momentum, gravity causes fall. 5.1.18.

Second Āhnika

Motion in Substances

1. नोदनाभिघातात् संयुक्तसंयोगाच्च पृथिव्यां कर्म ॥५।२।१॥

nodanābhighātāt saṃyuktasaṃyogācca pṛthivyāṃ karma ॥5.2.1॥

Force and impact jointly add to the pṛthivī's motion. 5.2.1.

The motion of a solid (the atom pṛthivī or gross matter) needs a force.

2. तत् विशेषेणादृष्टकारितम् ॥५।२।२॥

tat viśeṣenādṛṣṭakāritam ॥5.2.2॥

That [earthquake and similar movement] is caused by the hidden. 5.2.2.

But certain events are a consequence of a hidden chain of events and processes as in the case of an earthquake.

3. अपां संयोगाभावे गुरुत्वात् पतनम् ॥५।२।३॥

apāṃ saṃyogābhāve gurutvāt patanam ॥5.2.3॥

In liquids, falling down results from gravitation in the absence of conjunction. 5.2.3.

Gravitation is the ubiquitous force at the basis of flow.

4. द्रवत्वात् स्यन्दनम् ॥५।२।४॥

dravatvāt syandanam ॥5.2.4॥

Fluidity is the mechanism of the flow. 5.2.4.

But the nature of the flow depends on the viscosity of the fluid which depends on the thickness of the molecules of the fluid. Thus honey has a higher viscosity than water. In a channel, the particles of water flow faster on the surface than lower down.

5. नाड्यो वायुसंयोगादारोहणम् ॥५।२।५॥

nāḍyo vāyusaṃyogādārohaṇam ॥5.2.5॥

The sun's rays, with vāyu conjoined, [cause] the rise [of water]. 5.2.5.

Water is transported up the stem of a plant by tension caused by evaporation at the leaves which creates low pressure in the xylem that sucks up water from the high pressure environment at the base.

6. नोदनापीडनात् संयुक्तसंयोगाञ्च ॥५।२।६॥

nodanāpiḍanāt saṃyuktasaṃyogāñca ॥5.2.6॥

By the force [of the sunrays] transformed and jointly [with vāyu] conjoined [is the rise of water]. 5.2.6.

The rate of evaporation will be a determinative factor in the rate of the rise of water.

7. वृक्षाभिसर्पणमित्यदृष्टकारितम् ॥५।२।७॥

vṛkṣābhisarpaṇamityadṛṣṭakāritam ॥5.2.7॥

[In] the trees the circulation [of water] is caused by subtle [processes]. 5.2.7.

There are other subtle forces at work that cause water to circulate in the limbs of the tree.

8. अपां सङ्घातो विलयनञ्च तेजः संयोगात् ॥५।२।८॥

apāṃ saṅghāto vilayanañca tejaḥ saṃyogāt ॥5.2.8॥

The water's freezing and melting is from conjunction with tejas. 5.2.8.

The taking away of the tejas atoms from water will cause it to freeze and supply of more such atoms in the frozen state will cause it to melt.

9. तत्र विस्फूर्जथुर्लिङ्गम् ॥५।२।९॥

tatra visphūrjathurliṅgam ॥5.2.9॥

There the thunder [with the lightening] marks [the flow of tejas]. 5.2.9.

Tejas in the water causes lightening and the śabda of thunder.

10. वैदिकञ्च ॥५।२।१०॥

vaidikañca ॥5.2.10॥

And [so described] in the Vedas. 5.2.10.

The Vedas have the story that Agni takes refuge in the waters of the cloud.

11. अपां संयोगाद्विभागाच्च स्तनयित्नोः ॥५।२।११॥

apāṃ saṃyogādvibhāgācca stanayitnoḥ ॥5.2.11॥

The water in conjunction and disjunction in the clouds [causes electricity]. 5.2.11.

This conjunction and disjunction releases tejas that represents lightening and this process causes the sound of thunder.

12. पृथिवीकर्मणा तेजः कर्म वायुकर्म च व्याख्यातम् ॥५।२।१२॥

pṛthivīkarmaṇā tejaḥ karma vāyukarma ca vyākhyātam ॥5.2.12॥

In pṛthivī's activity, the tejas motion and the vāyu motion is explained [as the basis]. 5.2.12.

In an earthquake (which is pṛthivī's activity in the large scale) the responsible agents are motion underground caused by tejas and vāyu elements.

13. अग्नेरूर्ध्वज्वलनं वायोस्तिर्य्यक्पवनमणूनां मनसश्र्चाद्यं कर्मादृष्टकारितम् ॥५।२।१३॥

agnerūrdhvajvalanaṃ vāyostiryyakpavanamaṇūnāṃ manasaścādyaṃ karmādṛṣṭakāritam ॥5.2.13॥

The fire flaming upward, sideward blowing of air, and the initial movement of mind are caused by hidden [processes]. 5.2.13.

There are hidden processes (at a more elemental level) that explain the characteristics mentioned.

14. हस्तकर्मणा मनसः कर्म व्याख्यातम् ॥५।२।१४॥

hastakarmaṇā manasaḥ karma vyākhyātam ॥5.2.14॥

In the action of the hand the action of the mind is described. 5.2.14.

The choice of moving the hand is made in the mind.

15. आत्मेन्द्रियमनोऽर्थसन्निकर्षात् सुखदुःखे ॥५।२।१५॥

ātmendriyamano'rthasannikarṣāt sukhaduḥkhe ॥5.2.15॥

By the conjunction of the ātman, the senses, the mind, and the object pleasure and pain [are experienced]. 5.2.15.

The subjective experience of pleasure and pain are associated with the conjunction of the senses, the objects, and the ātman.

16. तदनारम्भ आत्मस्थे मनसि शरीरस्य दुःखाभावः स योगः ॥५।२।१६॥

tadanārambha ātmasthe manasi śarīrasya duḥkhābhāvaḥ sa yogaḥ ॥5.2.16॥

The non-origination of that [pleasure and pain] when the mind is steady in the ātman, resulting in the absence of the body's pain is yoga. 5.2.16.

When the body is steady in the ātman, there is a withdrawal both from the senses and the object of the senses leading to detachment and this is yoga.

17. अपसर्पणमुपसर्पणमशितपीतसंयोगाः
कार्यान्तरसंयोगाश्चेत्यदृष्टकारितानि ॥५।२।१७॥

apasarpaṇamusarpaṇamaśitapītasaṃyogāḥ
kāryāntarasaṃyogāścetyadṛṣṭakāritāni ॥5.2.17॥

The going out, the coming in, conjunctions of what is eaten and drunk, and conjunction of other actions are caused by the subtle. 5.2.17.

The specifics related to occurrences in life (including the entry and departure of life force in the body) are caused by a multitude of forces that are not always apparent.

18. तदभावे संयोगाभावेऽप्रादुर्भावश्च मोक्षः ॥५।२।१८॥

tadabhāve saṃyogābhāve'prādurbhāvaśca mokṣaḥ ॥5.2.18॥

The absence of that conjunction and non-recurrence [of the same] is said to be mokṣa (liberation). 5.2.18.

When the conjunctions do not occur, the individual is free of the causal chains connected to the past and so has obtained mokṣa.

19. द्रव्यगुणकर्मनिष्पत्तिवैधर्म्यादभावस्तमः ॥५।२।१९॥

dravyaguṇakarmaniṣpattivaidharmyādabhāvastamaḥ ॥5.2.19॥

The absence of substance, attribute, and action is the absence of [tejas] or [the presence of] darkness. 5.2.19.

The absence of light or tejas is not a substance even though shadows move.

20. तेजसो द्रव्यान्तरेणावरणाञ्च ॥५।२।२०॥

tejaso dravyāntareṇāvaraṇāñca ॥5.2.20॥

[Darkness is] also by the obscuring of light by another substance. 5.2.20.

The obscuring points to the unique properties of the tejas atoms.

21. दिक्कालावाकाशञ्च क्रियावद्वैधर्म्यान्निष्क्रियाणि ॥५।२।२१॥

dikkālāvākāśañca kriyāvaddhairmyānniṣkriyāṇi ॥5.2.21॥

Space, time and ākāśa differ from those which possess physical motion by lacking motion. 5.2.21.

Continuing the discussion of darkness (which is unembodied) as an entity, Kaṇāda says that space, time and ākāśa work differently for unembodied objects.

22. एतेन कर्माणि गुणाश्च व्याख्याताः ॥५।२।२२॥

etena karmāṇi guṇāśca vyākhyātāḥ ॥5.2.22॥

By these karman and qualities are explained. 5.2.22.

Thus we can understand how the physics of embodied objects cannot apply to un-embodied objects.

23. निष्क्रियाणां समवायः कर्मभ्यो निषिद्धः ।५।२।२३॥

niṣkriyāṇāṃ samavāyaḥ karmabhyo niṣiddhaḥ ॥5.2.23॥

The coinherence of non-dynamic entities is excluded from action. 5.2.23.

Unembodied objects cannot be dynamic. This may appear obvious but Kaṇāda is trying to build a logical system that applies to different substances and he is trying to establish that a non-substance must be considered different from an atomic substance like the four fundamental atoms.

24. कारणन्त्वसमवायिनो गुणाः ।५।२।२४॥

kāraṇantvasamavāyino guṇāḥ ॥5.2.24॥

Cause is that in which the qualities do not inhere. 5.2.24.

This presents the point that cause itself cannot be associated with qualities.

25. गुणैर्दिग्व्याख्याता ॥५।२।२५॥

guṇairdigvyākhyātā ॥5.2.25॥

By qualities space is explained. 5.2.25.

Space is to be described in terms of relationship between different objects. This relationship requires measurement which, in turn, may bring in the question of time associated with the measurements.

26. कारणेन कालः ॥५।२।२६॥

kāraṇena kālaḥ ॥5.2.26॥

Time is [defined] by way of causality. 5.2.26.

Time is described as the basis of causality. However space and time are dravyas and their qualities can mutually influence each other as in varying flows of time for different observers.

CHAPTER 6
First Āhnika

On Virtues

This chapter lists instructions for the students of the Vaiśeṣika. This is important because of the assumption that the ātman, who is ultimately the source of all knowledge, resides within each individual. The idea of education is to light the lamp of discrimination within the student's mind rather than fill the mind's vessel with information. In this, it is rather different from the model of education used in most modern academies.

1. बुद्धिपूर्वा वाक्यकृतिर्वेदे ॥६।१।१॥

buddhipūrvā vākyakṛtirvede ‖6.1.1‖

Understanding is preceded by sentence formation in the Veda. 6.1.1.

One must not look at isolated phrases for correct meaning. Also, it is important to analyze statements properly so as to arrive at the correct inference and also discover where the analysis leads to the falsity of the premise.

2. ब्राह्मणे संज्ञाकर्म सिद्धिलिङ्गम् ॥६।१।२॥

brāhmaṇe saṃjñākarma siddhiliṅgam ‖6.1.2‖

In the Brāhmaṇa (part of the Veda), designation and motion signify comprehension. 6.1.2.

This refers to the traditional discipline regarding the learning of the Veda directly and its commentary subsequently.

3. बुद्धिपूर्वो ददातिः ॥६।१।३॥

buddhipūrvo dadātiḥ ॥6.1.3॥

Prior to understanding is the giving. 6.1.3.

This concerns the importance of character (here, generosity) in intellectual and spiritual studies. Character is important for learning. Generosity in one's behavior is conducive to obtaining knowledge.

4. तथा प्रतिग्रहः ॥६।१।४॥

tathā pratigrahaḥ ॥6.1.4॥

Likewise that of the receiving. 6.1.4.

Humility is important because the excellent student knows that knowledge springs from within and the student must act as a prepared vessel.

5. आत्मान्तरगुणानामात्मान्तरऽकारणत्वात् ॥६।१।५॥

ātmāntaraguṇānāmātmāntara'kāraṇatvāt ॥6.1.5॥

The difference in qualities among individuals is not from causes in other individuals. 6.1.5.

The difference in experience is not to be explained merely by life events. Rather it is to be seen in the qualities that the experiencers have.

6. तद्दुष्टभोजने न विद्यते ॥६।१।६॥

taddusṭabhojane na vidyate ॥6.1.6॥

That [difference] does not arise from bad food. 6.1.6.

The difference is not from what one eats.

7. दुष्टं हिंसायाम् ॥६।१।७॥

duṣṭaṃ hiṃsāyām ॥6.1.7॥

The evil is in violence. 6.1.7.

The violence may not be physical alone and going against the higher law also constitutes violence.

8. तस्य समभिव्याहारतो दोषः॥६।१।८॥

tasya samabhivyāhārato doṣaḥ ॥6.1.8॥

From [bad] company comes evil. 6.1.8.

Experience has an interactional component and the bad can lead others astray.

9. तददुष्टे न विद्यते॥६।१।९॥

tadaduṣṭe na vidyate ॥6.1.9॥

That is not known in one with no bad [qualities]. 6.1.9.

But social interaction with a good person is to be valued.

10. पुनर्विशिष्टे प्रवृत्तिः॥६।१।१०॥

punarviśiṣṭe pravṛttiḥ ॥6.1.10॥

Again [it explains] the origin of the worthy. 6.1.10.

11. समे हीने वा प्रवृत्तिः॥६।१।११॥

same hīne vā pravṛttiḥ ॥6.1.11॥

The origin of the equal and the inferior. 6.1.11.

This means that the character of individuals forms a spectrum.

12. एतेन हीनसमविशिष्टधार्मिकेभ्यः परस्वादानं व्याख्यातम्॥६।१।१२॥

etena hīnasamaviśiṣṭadhārmikebhyaḥ parasvādānaṃ vyākhyātam ॥6.1.12॥

By these the reception in the association among [those in] inferior, equal and superior paths is explained. 6.1.12.

The multiplicity in character explains why one must deal with people according to circumstance.

13. तथा विरुद्धानां त्यागः॥६।१।१३॥

tathā viruddhānāṃ tyāgaḥ ॥6.1.13॥

Likewise, reject those who are opposed [to knowledge]. 6.1.13.

And even reject those who are unworthy or opposed to the right way. Indeed there are times when one must fight as in the case of tyranny.

14. हीने परे त्यागः ॥६।१।१४॥

hīne pare tyāgaḥ ॥6.1.14॥

One may withdraw from the inferior. 6.1.14.

This means that one may not compel one who is not prepared to partake in the learning of the science of matter, mind and consciousness.

15. समे आत्मत्यागः परत्यागो वा॥६।१।१५॥

same ātmatyāgaḥ paratyāgo vā ॥6.1.15॥

Among the equal, the rejection of the other is the rejection of one's own ātman. 6.1.15.

But for those who are prepared, it should be the goal to spread this learning.

16. विशिष्टे आत्मत्याग इति॥६।१।१६॥

viśiṣṭe ātmatyāga iti ॥6.1.16॥

Among the superior, rejecting [is like rejecting] one's own ātman; such is the way. 6.1.16.

And the same is true for other discerning individuals who do not know of the way.

Second Āhnika

Deeds with Seen and Unseen Fruits

1. दृष्टादृष्टप्रयोजनानां दृष्टाभावे प्रयोजनमभ्युदयाय॥६।२।१॥

dṛṣṭādṛṣṭaprayojanānāṃ dṛṣṭābhāve prayojanamabhyudayāya ॥6.2.1॥

Among the purposes of actions [with fruit] that is seen or unseen, [and in spite of] the absence of the seen [fruit], the objective is enlightenment. 6.2.1.

The purpose of learning is enlightenment, that is the attainment of self-knowledge.

2. अभिषेचनोपवासब्रह्मचर्यगुरुकुलवासवानप्रस्थ यज्ञदानप्रोक्षणदिङ्नक्षत्रकालनियमाश्चादृष्टाय॥६।२।२॥

abhiṣecanopavāsabrahmacaryagurukulavāsavānaprasthayajñadānaprokṣaṇadiṅnakṣatrakālaniyamāścādṛṣṭāya ॥6.2.2॥

Consecration, fasting, sacred studies, schooling, forest dwelling, sacrifice, alms, sprinkling water, watching stars and time, and observations are for the unseen [fruits]. 6.2.2.

These observations and disciplines prepare the seeker for understanding as they include reflection that leads to an apprehension of the counter-intuitive aspects of reality and experience.

On Anupadhā or Faith

3. चातुराश्रम्यमुपधा अनुपधाश्व॥६।२।३॥

cāturāśramyamupadhā anupadhāśva ॥6.2.3॥

And the four stage system of life, without faith and with faith too. 6.2.3.

The seeker lives in the four-stage system of life, with or without faith.

4. भावदोष उपधाऽदोषऽनुपधा॥६।२।४॥

bhāvadoṣa upadhā'doṣa'nupadhā ॥6.2.4॥

Lack of faith in becoming is upadhā, and faith is anupadhā. 6.2.4.

Mechanical life is one of upadhā whereas mindful life denoted anupadhā or faith.

5. यदिष्टरूपरसगन्धस्पर्शं प्रोक्षितमभ्युक्षितञ्च तच्छशुचि॥६।२।५॥

yadiṣṭarūparasagandhasparśaṃ prokṣitamabhyukṣitañca tacchaśuci ॥6.2.5॥

That which has touch, taste, smell in a desired form and is sprinkled with water is virtuous. 6.2.5.

Now ritual is explained. Not every moment can be mindful and there is much that must remain as is custom. The idea of virtuous ritual is activity that purifies the four atomic elements within. This purification is in the sense of removing coverings that obscure inner sense.

6. अशुचीति शुचिप्रतिषेधः ॥६।२।६॥

aśucīti śucipratiṣedhaḥ ॥6.2.6॥

Non-virtue is the form of negation of virtue. 6.2.6.

7. अर्थान्तरञ्च ॥६।२।७॥

arthāntarañca ॥6.2.7॥

Also the other [non-virtuous śabda]. 6.2.7.

Bad speech can also lead to non-virtue.

8. अयतस्य शुचिभोजनादभ्युदयो न विद्यते नियमाभावात् विद्यते वाऽर्थान्तरत्वाद् यमस्य॥६।२।८॥

ayatasya śucibhojanādabhyudayo na vidyate niyamābhāvāt vidyate vā'rthāntaratvād yamasya ॥6.2.8॥

For the unrestrained, enlightenment does not come from eating virtuous food [and other virtuous actions]; lack of restraints leads not to concomitant facilitators of discipline. 6.2.8.

Outwardly virtuous life is not enough; one needs disciplined life to be able to arrive at understanding.

9. असति च अभावात् ॥६।२।९॥

asati ca abhāvāt ॥6.2.9॥

Non-reality is from non-existence. 6.2.9.

Asat is a sense of reality that is divorced from physical and psychological facts. It arises from wrong passions, like that of one who harms or kills without justification.

10. सुखाद्रागः ॥६।२।१०॥

sukhādrāgaḥ ॥6.2.10॥

From pleasure longing [arises]. 6.2.10.

11. तन्मयत्वाञ्च॥६।२।११॥

tanmayatvāñca ॥6.2.11॥

And from the absorption [in it], impressions. 6.2.11.

These impressions lead one to attachment and aversion.

12. अदृष्टाञ्च॥६।२।१२॥

adṛṣṭāñca ॥6.2.12॥

[Caused] by the subtle. 6.2.12.

Other subtle impressions also lead to attachment and aversion.

13. जातिविशेषाञ्च॥६।२।१३॥

jātiviśeṣāñca ॥6.2.13॥

And by the particularity of the class. 6.2.13.

Still others arise out of the intrinsic nature of the individuals being considered whether they are human or animal.

14. इच्छाद्वेषपूर्विका धर्माधर्मप्रवृत्तिः ॥६।२।१४॥

icchādveṣapūrvikā dharmādharmapravṛttiḥ ॥6.2.14॥

Desire and aversion [as activity] precede the inclinations of righteousness and non-righteousness. 6.2.14.

15. तत्संयोगो विभागः ॥६।२।१५॥

tatsaṃyogo vibhāgaḥ ॥6.2.15॥

That is [explained by] conjunction and disjunction. 6.2.15.

16. आत्मकर्मसु मोक्षो व्याख्यातः ॥६।२।१६॥

ātmakarmasu mokṣo vyākhyātaḥ ॥6.2.16॥

In the action of the ātman is liberation described. 6.2.16.

CHAPTER 7

First Āhnika

Universal and Transient Qualities

1. उक्ता गुणाः ॥७।१।१॥

uktā guṇāḥ ॥7.1.1॥

Qualities are [now] addressed. 7.1.1.

We return to the category of qualities that is one amongst the six representing ontological reality.

2. पृथिव्यादिरूपरसगन्धस्पर्शा द्रव्यानित्यत्वादनित्याश्च ॥७।१।२॥

pṛthivyādirūparasagandhasparśā dravyānityatvādanityāśca ॥7.1.2॥

[Beginning with the dravya] pṛthivī, [the qualities] color, taste, odor and touch are also non-eternal because of the non-eternality of the dravyas. 7.1.2.

The qualities apprehended by the senses are not eternal for the substrate elements are not eternal.

3. एतेन नित्येषु नित्यत्वमुक्तम् ॥७।१।३॥

etena nityeṣu nityatvamuktam ॥7.1.3॥

By this [the opposite of] the eternality in eternals is explained. 7.1.3.

This implies that eternal dravyas have qualities that are eternal.

4. अप्सु तेजसि वायौ च नित्या द्रव्यनित्यत्वात् ॥७।१।४॥

apsu tejasi vayau ca nityā dravyanityatvāt ॥7.1.4॥

Āpas, tejas and vāyu are eternal from the eternality of the [atoms in the corresponding] dravyas. 7.1.4.

Śaṅkara Miśra explains that in āpas atoms form, taste, and touch qualities are eternal; in tejas atoms form and touch are eternal; and in vāyu atoms touch is eternal.

5. अनित्येष्वनित्या द्रव्यानित्यत्वात्॥७।१।५॥

anityeṣvanityā dravyānityatvāt ॥7.1.5॥

Non-eternality in the non-eternal is a consequence of the non-eternality of the substrate. 7.1.5.

6. कारणगुणपूर्वकाः पृथिव्यां पाकजाः॥ ७।१।६॥

kāraṇaguṇapūrvakāḥ pṛthivyāṃ pākajāḥ ॥7.1.6॥

The causative agent for the emergence of qualities in pṛthivī is heat. 7.1.6.

The emergence of the qualities necessitates an interaction between pṛthivī and tejas atoms.

7. एक द्रव्यत्वात् ॥७।१।७॥

eka dravyatvāt ॥7.1.7॥

From one dravya as a substrate. 7.1.7.

The qualities that the pṛthivī material shows is a consequence of the catalysis by the tejas atoms.

Atomicity and Wholeness

8. अणोर्महतश्चोपलब्ध्यनुपलब्धी नित्ये व्याख्याते ॥७।१।८॥

aṇormahataścopalabdhyanupalabdhī nitye vyākhyāte ॥7.1.8॥

The recognition and non-recognition of atom's extension is explained in eternals. 7.1.8.

This discussion was done earlier in chapter 4.

9. कारणबहुत्वाञ्च ॥७।१।९॥

kāraṇabahutvāñca ॥7.1.9॥

And the cause is from multiplicity [of atoms]. 7.1.9.

The explanation of extension is multiplicity.

10. अतोविपरीतमणु ॥७।१।१०॥

atoviparītamaṇu ॥7.1.10॥

Of this, the contrary is the aṇu.7.1.10.

The atom, on the other hand, is by itself.

11. अणु महदिति तस्मिन् विशेषभावात् विशेषाभावाच्च ॥७।१।११॥

aṇu mahaditi tasmin viśeṣābhāvāt viśeṣābhāvācca ॥7.1.11॥

The difference [of the behavior] in the small and the large [in cases] derives from the particularity [of the larger magnitude] and not from the non-particularity [of the atom's magnitude]. 7.1.11.

But the behavior of the large has associated with it particularity arising out of the structure of the physical system even though the constituent atoms do not have particularity amongst their qualities.

12. एककालत्वात् ॥७।१।१२॥

ekakālatvāt ॥7.1.12॥

From momentariness in time. 7.1.12.

Furthermore, the properties of the collective are distinct due to the large duration over which the collective is observed and that of the atom due to the short duration of its examination.

13. दृष्टान्ताच्च ॥७।१।१३॥

dṛṣṭāntācca ॥7.1.13॥

By perspective as well. 7.1.13.

The distinction between the collective and the atom is enhanced by the perspective of the observation.

14. अणुत्वमहत्वयोरणुत्वमहत्वाभावः कर्मगुणैर्व्याख्यातः ॥७।१।१४॥

aṇutvamahatvayoraṇutvamahatvābhāvaḥ

karmaguṇairvyākhyātaḥ ॥7.1.14॥

The non-absence of atomicity in atoms and wholeness in collective is explained by motion and qualities. 7.1.14.

Thus wholeness of the collective is an emergent property.

15. कर्मभिः कर्माणि गुणैश्चगुणा व्याख्यातः ॥७।१।१५॥

karmabhiḥ karmāṇi guṇaiścaguṇā vyākhyātaḥ ॥7.1.15॥

From the motions [observed] motion, and from the qualities [observed] quality are described. 7.1.15.

The motions and the properties of the constituent atoms are ultimately aggregated in new ways in the motions and properties of the collective.

16. अणुत्वमहत्वाभ्यां कर्मगुणाश्च व्याख्यातः ॥७।१।१६॥

aṇutvamahatvābhyāṃ karmaguṇāśca vyākhyātaḥ ॥7.1.16॥

From aṇutva and mahatva, motion and qualities are described.7.1.16.

The emergent properties of the collective are termed mahatva whereas the property of the atom is due to aṇutva.

17. एतेन दीर्घत्वह्रस्वत्वे व्याख्याते ॥७।१।१७॥

etena dīrghatvahrasvatve vyākhyāte ॥7.1.17॥

By these the largeness and the smallness are described. 7.1.17.

Thus aggregate matter comes to have new properties that were not apparent in the constituent atoms.

18. अनित्येऽनित्यम्॥७।१।१८॥

anitye'nityaṃ ॥7.1.18॥

In the anitya [dravyas the above qualities are] anitya. 7.1.18.

Naturally, the properties are non-eternal if the substance is non-eternal and vice versa as in the next sūtra.

19. नित्ये नित्यम्॥७।१।१९॥

nitye nityaṃ ॥7.1.19॥

[These qualities are] eternal (nitya) in eternals.7.1.19.

20. नित्यं परिमण्डलम् ॥७।१।२०॥

nityaṃ parimaṇḍalam ॥7.1.20॥

The roundness [of the atom] is universal. 7.1.20.

This is the argument for the roundness of the atom.

21. अविद्या च विद्यालिङ्गम् ॥७।१।२१॥

avidyā ca vidyāliṅgam ॥7.1.21॥

Ignorance too signifies [the existence of] knowledge. 7.1.21.

The lack of a property also leads to a deeper understanding of the object.

Size of Ākāśa, Mind, Space, and Time

22. विभवान्महानाकाशस्तथा चात्मा ॥७।१।२२॥

vibhavānmahānākāśastathā cātmā ॥7.1.22॥

Immense is the expanse of ākāśa and that of the ātman. 7.1.22.

The ākāśa is the continuous substrate that makes it possible for a field to exist and its immensity denotes that it is infinite. The immensity of ātman is not related to the nature of space and time for it is a different dravya. Nevertheless, ātman informs the manas and makes cognitions possible.

23. तदभावादणु मनः ॥७।१।२३॥

tadabhāvādaṇu manaḥ ॥7.1.23॥

Owing to the absence of that, mind is atomic. 7.1.23.

Although manas is also eternal, it is atomic. This leads to the question of how the ātman and the manas form a conjunction. Unlike ākāśa, the ātman does not need space and time for support. The conjunction is therefore limited by the further conjunction with the citta (memory) structures available to the manas.

There exist many different neural correlates of different kinds of consciousnesses, which idea is supported by the fact that there are specialized modules for particular perceptions. Furthermore, conscious experience is selective: some neural activity generates it whereas other activity doesn't. If consciousness is equated to attention, there appears to be greater overlap between mechanisms of memory and awareness than between those of attention and awareness. When considered as activity in specific areas of the brain, consciousness appears to depend on the activity in thalamus and brain stem, or in higher prefrontal and parietal association areas. The claustrum, in the underside of the neocortex, has also been identified as the region where widespread coordination of the activity occurs resulting in the seamless quality of conscious experience; the claustrum synchronizes the activity between both the cortical hemispheres and between cortical regions within the same hemisphere.

If we consider language, the complex manner in which aphasias manifest establishes that its production and processing is a tangled process. Certain components of the language functioning process operate in a binary fashion. These components include comprehension, production, repetition, and various abstract processes. Viewing each as a separate module is not quite correct due to subtle interrelationships mediating between these capabilities which all come into operation in normal behavior. The explanation of counterintuitive disorders such as alexia without agraphia can only be understood by postulating decision nodes that do not have physical neural correlates.

From the point of view of anesthesia, two states of consciousness may be postulated for the patient who is not fully anesthetized: (i) the patient seems to be cognizant responding to commands but with no postoperative recall or memory of the events; and, (ii) the patient can recall events postoperatively, but was not necessarily conscious enough to respond to commands. Our understanding of these cases must be addressed by the model of consciousness states that is developed, and reconciled with the hierarchy of conscious, preconscious, and subliminal processing that is well understood.

24. गुणैर्दिग् व्याख्याता ॥७।१।२४॥

guṇardig vyākhyātā ॥7.1.24॥

In qualities, space is described. 7.1.24.

25. कारणे कालः ॥७।१।२५॥

kāraṇe kālaḥ ॥7.1.25॥

In cause, time. 7.1.25.

Second Āhnika

Unity and Discreteness

1. रूपरसगन्धस्पर्शव्यतिरेकादर्थान्तरमेकत्वम् ॥७।२।१॥

rūparasagandhasparśavyatirekādarthāntaramekatvam ॥7.2.1॥

Form, touch, taste and odor in their multiplicity indicate the existence of wholeness. 7.2.1.

Wholeness is a property that binds a collective together.

2. तथा पृथक्त्वम् ॥७।२।२॥

tathā pṛthaktvam ॥7.2.2॥

Likewise discreteness. 7.2.2.

A whole structure is also discrete.

3. एकत्वैकपृथक्त्वयोरेकत्वैकपृथक्त्वाभावोऽणुत्वमहत्वाभ्यां व्याख्यातः ॥७।२।३॥

ekatvaikapṛthaktvayorekatvaikapṛthaktvābhāvo'ṇutvamahat vābhyāṃ vyākhyātaḥ ॥7.2.3॥

The non-existence of wholeness and discreteness in wholeness and discreteness is explained by atomicity and extension. 7.2.3.

This means that wholeness and discreteness are not universal concepts. Thus the wholeness of one object may be very different from the wholeness of another object, just as the discreteness of a proton is very different from the discreteness of an electron.

4. निःसंख्यत्वात् कर्मगुणानां सर्वैकत्वं न विद्यते ॥७।२।४॥

niḥsaṃkhyatvāt karmaguṇānām sarvaikatvaṃ na vidyate ॥7.2.4॥

[Being] void of numbers, action and qualities do not support wholeness in all [categories]. 7.2.4.

Wholeness is not thus contingent on specific counts. Specificity of count is a quality and any single quality cannot be the basis for wholeness for in action a whole is not contingent on any count.

5. भ्रान्तं तत् ॥७।२।५॥

bhrāntaṃ tat ॥7.2.5॥

That [unified view] is erroneous. 7.2.5.

Since qualities cannot reside in qualities, the view that wholeness can be based on number is erroneous.

6. एकत्वाभावाद्भक्तिस्तु न विद्यते ॥७।२।६॥

ekatvābhāvādbhaktistu na vidyate ॥7.2.6॥

From the absence of wholeness [in number], its further division is not known. 7.2.6.

A whole cannot be further divided into wholes.

7. कार्यकारणयोरेकत्वैकपृथक्त्वाभावदेकत्वैकपृथक्त्वं न विद्यते ॥७।२।७॥

kāryakāraṇayorekatvaikapṛthaktvābhāvadekatvaikapṛthaktvam na vidyate ॥7.2.7॥

From the absence of wholeness and discreteness in physical motion and cause, [their] wholeness and discreteness are not known. 7.2.7.

Physical motion and forces can be subdivided for they are not whole.

8. एतदनित्ययोर्व्याख्यातम् ॥७।२।८॥

etadanityayorvyākhyātam ॥7.2.8॥

This has been explained in non-eternals. 7.2.8.

Thus non-discrete variables can vary.

Conjunction and Disjunction

9. अन्यतरकर्मज उभयकर्मजः संयोगजश्च संयोगः ।७।२।९॥

anyatarakarmaja ubhayakarmajaḥ saṃyogajaśca saṃyogaḥ ॥7.2.9॥

Conjunction results from one [out of two substances] in motion, both being in motion, and from conjunction as well. 7.2.9.

Conjunction can occur in a variety of ways depending on the motions of the constitutive objects.

10. एतेन विभागो व्याख्यातः ॥७।२।१०॥

etena vibhāgo vyākhyātaḥ ॥7.2.10॥

By these disjunction is explained. 7.2.10.

And that is also the basis of dravyas coming apart in disjunction.

11. संयोगविभागयोः संयोगविभागाभावोऽणुत्वमहत्वाभ्यां व्याख्यातः ॥७।२।११॥

saṃyogavibhāgayoḥ saṃyogavibhāgābhāvo'ṇutvamahatvābhyāṃ vyākhyātaḥ ॥7.2.11॥

The non-existence of conjunction and disjunction in conjunction and disjunction is explained by atomicity and extension. 7.2.11.

This is a point related to the terminology. Śaṅkara Miśra says: "Just as an atom and a great whole do not have another atom or great whole as substrate, conjunction and disjunction do not have conjunction and disjunction as qualities."

12. कर्मभिः कर्माणि गुणैर्गुणा अणुत्वमहत्वाभ्यामिति॥७।२।१२॥

karmabhiḥ karmāṇi guṇairguṇā aṇutvamahatvābhyāmiti ॥7.2.12॥

The non-existence of karman in karman and attribute in qualities is explained by atomicity and extension. 7.2.12.

Just as another atom cannot be a part of an atom and a whole be a part of a whole, karman cannot be in karman and quality in quality.

13. युतसिद्ध्यभावात् कार्यकारणयोः संयोगविभागौ न विद्यते ॥७।२।१३॥

yutasiddhyabhāvāt kāryakāraṇayoḥ saṃyogavibhāgau na vidyate ॥7.2.13॥

From the absence of discreteness in cause and physical motion, conjunction and disjunction are absent [in them]. 7.2.13.

This is again a clarification of the terminology related to conjunction and disjunction.

14. गुणत्वात्॥७।२।१४॥

guṇatvāt ॥7.2.14॥

From being a quality. 7.2.14.

This is a continuation of the earlier sūtra on the absence of conjunction and disjunction as a quality in physical motion.

15. गुणोऽपि विभाव्यते॥७।२।१५॥

guṇo'pi vibhāvyate ॥7.2.15॥

Qualities are also described. 7.2.15.

This description is in words but the description is in a metalanguage so that the work need not have the same characteristics as the quality it represents.

16. निष्क्रियत्वात् ॥७।२।१६॥

niṣkriyatvāt ॥7.2.16॥

From lack of motion. 7.2.16.

Thus the word for motion itself cannot move.

17. असति नास्तीति च प्रयोगात् ॥७।२।१७॥

asati nāstīti ca prayogāt ॥7.2.17॥

In the absence [of the category], this is not so in the use [of the term]. 7.2.17.

A thing may be mentioned about a place without implying that it exists there because one may be speaking of the absence or its presence at a future time or in the past.

18. शब्दार्थावसम्बन्धौ ॥७।२।१८॥

śabdārthāvasambandhau ॥7.2.18॥

The word and meaning are unrelated. 7.2.18.

The word and its meaning is not like the conjunction of two objects which is governed by physical laws. Meaning is, therefore, a matter of convention that arises from custom and usage.

19. संयोगिनो दण्डात् समवायिनो विशेषाच्च ॥७।२।१९॥

saṃyogino daṇḍāt samavāyino viśeṣācca ॥7.2.19॥

Conjunction from the staff and inherence from the particular. 7.2.19.

The conjunction of the staff with the man wielding it arises from the particularity of the relationship. Likewise, the conjunction of the trunk to the elephant arises from the particular quality associated with the animal.

20. सामयिकः शब्दार्थप्रत्ययः ॥७।२।२०॥

sāmayikaḥ śabdārthapratyayaḥ ॥7.2.20॥

The meaning of the word comes from the context. 7.2.20.

The context is apprehended by the manas. But manas is in contact with the ātman, so the agency of the latter is at work in obtaining the meaning of the word.

Apartness and Conjunction

21. एकदिक्काभ्यामेककालाभ्यां सन्निकृष्टविप्रकृष्टाभ्यां परमपरञ्च ॥७।२।२१॥

ekadikkābhyāmekakālābhyāṃ sannikṛṣṭaviprakṛṣṭābhyāṃ paramaparañca ॥7.2.21॥

Those situated in one place and one time, near or far, may be separated or conjoined. 7.2.21.

Apartness or conjunction would be determined by the respective motions of the objects.

22. कारणपरत्वात् कारणापरत्वाच्च ॥७।२।२२॥

kāraṇaparatvāt kāraṇāparatvācca ॥7.2.22॥

By cause apart, by cause together also. 7.2.22.

The mutual relationship between things is determined by the behavior of the dravya time. One may extend this to apply to the atoms in a jar and claim that any two atoms will be conjoined if the jar is observed for sufficient amount of time.

23. परत्वापरत्वयोः परत्वापरत्वाभावोऽणुत्वमहत्वाभ्यां व्याख्यातः ॥७।२।२३॥

paratvāparatvayoḥ paratvāparatvābhāvo'ṇutvamahattvābhyāṃ vyākhyātaḥ ॥7.2.23॥

The non-existence of apartness and conjunction in apartness and conjunction is explained by atomicity and extension. 7.2.23.

This is because these categories are not the same as the properties described just as atoms and wholes can never be together.

24. कर्मभिः कर्माणि ॥७।२।२४॥

karmabhiḥ karmāṇi ॥7.2.24॥

From karman karman [arises].7.2.24.

From motion only motion can arise for the padārthas are disjoint categories.

25. गुणैर्गुणाः ॥७।२।२५॥

guṇairguṇāḥ ॥7.2.25॥

From qualities qualities [arise]. 7.2.25.

The category guṇa for the same reason cannot produce other padārthas.

Inherence as a Dravya

26. इहेदमिति यतः कार्यकारणयोः स समवायः ॥७।२।२६॥

ihedamiti yataḥ kāryakāraṇayoḥ sa samavāyaḥ ॥7.2.26॥

From which "here" and "this" result in motion and cause that is inherence. 7.2.26.

Inherence (samavāya) is defined in terms of such coming together of things so that we can address them as "here" or "this".

27. द्रव्यत्वगुणत्वप्रतिषेधो भावेन व्याख्यातः ॥७।२।२७॥

dravyatvaguṇatvapratiṣedho bhāvena vyākhyātaḥ ॥7.2.27॥

The negation of dravyatva and guṇatva are explained by existence [sattā]. 7.2.27.

Existence (sattā) is prior to the apprehension of dravya and guṇa.

28. तत्वभावेन ॥७।२।२८॥

tattvabhāvena ॥7.2.28॥

Oneness is explained by its category [sattā] 7.2.28.

CHAPTER 8

First Āhnika

On Cognition

1. द्रव्येषु ज्ञानं व्याख्यातम् ॥८।१।१॥

dravyeṣu jñānam vyākhyātam ॥8.1.1॥

[In the chapter on] dravyas cognition is explained. 8.1.1.

Cognition, through the workings of the manas dravya was described in Chapter 3.

2. तत्रात्मा मनश्चाप्रत्यक्षे ॥८।१।२॥

tatrātmā manaścāpratyekṣe ॥8.1.2॥

There [among dravyas], the ātman and the manas are among the non-visible. 8.1.2.

This was explained by the fact that the ātman and the mind have no apprehendable qualities.

3. ज्ञाननिर्देशे ज्ञाननिष्पत्तिविधिरुक्तः ॥८।१।३॥

jñānanirdeśe jñānaniṣpattividhiruktaḥ ॥8.1.3॥

To disseminate knowledge, the process of the emergence of the knowledge [is needed], it is said. 8.1.3.

Knowledge is the process, involving linkages between various categories and dravyas, which leads to deeper intuition.

4. गुणकर्मसु सन्निकृष्टेषु ज्ञाननिष्पत्तेर्द्रव्यं कारणम् ॥८।१।४॥

guṇakarmasu sannikṛṣteṣu jñānaniṣpatterdravyaṃ kāraṇam ॥8.1.4॥

Dravya is the cause of the evolution of cognition, when attribute and motion are in proximity (of the senses of perception). 8.1.4.

The senses must be directed at the dravya for the cognition to arise.

5. सामान्यविशेषु सामान्यविशेषाभावात्तत एव ज्ञानम् ॥८।१।५॥

sāmānyaviśeṣu sāmānyaviśeṣābhāvāttat eva jñānam ॥8.1.5॥

In the absence of some universals and particulars, and presence of others, knowledge [arises]. 8.1.5.

Knowledge arises in a particular selection out of the many that are possible. The universal, by itself, does not convey information but in conjunction with the particular it does. The more the specificity (together with the unlikely nature of it), the greater the information. Thus something that is known to occur with complete certainty does not carry knowledge.

6. सामान्यविशेषापेक्षं द्रव्यगुणकर्मसु ॥८।१।६॥

sāmānyaviśeṣāpekṣaṃ dravyaguṇakarmasu ॥8.1.6॥

The cognition of universal and particular is among dravyas with attribute and motion. 8.1.6.

The dravyas must be in a state of motion, with apprehendable attributes. Cognition thus has a temporal aspect to it.

7. द्रव्ये द्रव्यगुणकर्मापेक्षम्॥८।१।७॥

dravye dravyaguṇakarmāpekṣam ॥8.1.7॥

In dravyas, [cognition arises from] anticipation of dravya, attribute and motion. 8.1.7.

Information is function of the difference between the anticipated and the actual. The universal has no information because its actual presence is precisely equal to its anticipated value.

8. गुणकर्मसु गुणकर्माभावाद्गगुणकर्मापेक्षं न विद्यते ॥८।१।८॥

guṇakarmasu guṇakarmābhāvādgaguṇakarmāpekṣaṃ na vidyate ॥8.1.8॥

From the absence of attribute and motion in attribute and motion, anticipation of attribute and motion is not known. 8.1.8.

This repeats the point that the description is different from the phenomenon it describes.

9. समवायिनः श्वैत्याच्छ्वैत्यबुद्धेश्च श्वेते बुद्धिस्ते एते कार्य्यकारणभूते ॥८।१।९॥

samavāyinaḥ śvaityācchavaityabuddheśca śvete buddhiste ete kāryyakāraṇabhute ||8.1.9||

The cognition [of a dravya] inhered with whiteness results from both the white attribute and the knowledge of whiteness, this is a case of cause and effect. 8.1.9.

The cognition of a quality requires first a discrimination of this specific quality from others as well as an intuition of this quality.

10. द्रव्येष्वनितरेतरकारणाः॥८।१।१०॥

dravyeṣvanitaretarakāraṇāḥ ||8.1.10||

Among dravyas, cognition is not a mutual cause. 8.1.10.

The cognition of one thing cannot lead to the cognition of other things since the basis of cognition is discrimination amongst the many that are known that cannot include others that are not known.

11. कारणायौगपध्यात् कारणक्रमाच्च घटपटादिबुद्धीनां क्रमो न हेतुफलभावात् ॥८।१।११॥

kāraṇāyaugapadhyāt kāraṇākramācca ghaṭapaṭādibuddhīnāṃ kramo na hetuphalabhāvāt ||8.1.11||

The temporal nature of cause, within the process, results in a sequence in the objects that is not from the cause and effect relation. 8.1.11.

The sequence of responses is generated by the temporal nature of causes.

Second Āhnika

Types of Knowledge

1. अयमेष त्वया कृतं भोजयैनमिति बुद्धयपेक्षम् ॥८।२।१॥

ayameṣa tvayā kṛtaṃ bhojayainamiti buddhayapekṣam ॥8.2.1॥

"This is", "he is", "by you", "done", "feed him", all these require cognition. 8.2.1.

Cognition requires an awareness of the other and its observation in specific location and time. Implicit in this is the distinction between the observer and the observed and the knowledge of this distinction is informed by knowledge of self and its relationship with other objects around which has a temporal aspect to it. The observer must, therefore, be defined both by an "I" (which is pure awareness) and a "me" (which is the autobiographical self).

2. दृष्टेषु भावाददृष्टेष्वभावात् ॥८।२।२॥

dṛṣṭeṣu bhāvādadṛṣṭeṣvabhāvāt ॥8.2.2॥

In the perceived [the cognition is] by feeling, and in the non-perceived by the absence of feeling. 8.2.2.

Cognition is based on input through the senses that is predicated on conjunction of different dravyas including those of space and time.

3. अर्थ इति द्रव्यगुणकर्मसु ॥८।२।३॥

artha iti dravyaguṇakarmasu ॥8.2.3॥

The cognition of an object is in dravya, attribute and physical motion. 8.2.3.

The cognition must join each of the nine dravyas together with karman and guṇa with the cognitive padārthas represented by sāmānya, viśeṣa, and samavāya.

4. द्रव्येषु पञ्चात्मकं प्रतिषिद्धम्॥८।२।४॥

dravyeṣu pañcātmakaṃ pratiṣiddham ॥8.2.4॥

Among dravyas, a five-element basis is prohibited. 8.2.4.

Compound dravyas cannot be decomposed into five elements because ākāśa is not atomic.

5. भूयस्त्वाद्गन्धवत्त्वाञ्च पृथिवी गन्धज्ञाने प्रकृतिः॥८।२।५॥

bhūyastvādgandhavattvāñca pṛthivī gandhajñāne prakṛtiḥ ॥8.2.5॥

Pṛthivī is in the cognition of smell because it evolves from its own parts and has the inhered attribute of smell in it. 8.2.5.

The aṇu's of pṛthivī are associated with the tanmātra of gandha which leads to the cognition of smell.

6. तथापस्तेजोवायुश्च रसरूपस्पर्शाविशेषात्॥८।२।६॥

tathāpastejovāyuśca rasarūpasparśāviśeṣāt ||8.2.6||

Likewise āpas, tejas and vāyu are associated with the particular senses of taste, form and touch. 8.2.6.

The mind uses these senses to apprehend the nature of the dravya associated with the atomic elements.

CHAPTER 9

First Āhnika

On Non-Existence

1. क्रियागुणव्यपदेशाभावात् प्रागसत् ॥९।१।१॥

kriyāguṇavyapadeśābhāvāt prāgasat ॥9.1.1॥

Preceding the process of activity and [transformation of] quality, and before the outcome, [there is] no reality. 9.1.1.

This implies that it is the process of activity and change and that of observation which creates reality as we understand it.

2. सदसत् ॥९।१।२॥

sadasat ॥9.1.2॥

Real [cannot be] unreal. 9.1.2.

Reality cannot be seen as illusive.

3. असतः क्रियागुणव्यपदेशाभावादर्थान्तरम् ॥९।१।३॥

asataḥ kriyāguṇavyapadeśābhāvādarthāntaram ॥9.1.3॥

The unreal due to the absence of detectable qualities or physical motion is a different object [compared to the real]. 9.1.3.

There exist virtual particles.

4. सच्चासत् ॥९।१।४॥

saccāsat ॥9.1.4॥

The real [is] unreal. 9.1.4.

The real of one time and place may not be true of another time and place.

5. यच्चान्यदसदतस्तदसत् ॥९।१।५॥

yaccānyadasadatastadasat ॥9.1.5॥

And that which is differently unreal from these is unreal. 9.1.5.

Yet there are other conceptions (different from the above) that are fully unreal.

6. असदिति भूतप्रत्यक्षाभावात् भूतस्मृतेर्विरोधिप्रत्यक्षवत् ॥९।१।६॥

asiditi bhūtapratyakṣābhāvāt bhūtasmṛtervirodhipratyakṣavat ॥9.1.6॥

The destruction of an existing object and the memory of a previously existing object are also unreal. 9.1.6.

Reality is defined in time with respect to the observer.

7. तथाऽभावे भावप्रत्यक्षत्वाञ्च ॥९।१।७॥

tathā'bhāve bhāvapratyakṣatvāñca ॥9.1.7॥

And in the absence [of destruction], the feeling of being is experienced. 9.1.7.

The embodied universe is an expression of being, so truly experiencing any instances of it brings us to it.

8. एतेनाघटोऽगौरधर्मश्च व्याख्यातः ॥९।१।८॥

etenāghaṭo'gauradharmaśca vyākhyātaḥ ॥9.1.8॥

By this [examples of differences] in pots, cows, or duties are also explained. 9.1.8.

The differences in understanding arise out of flawed memories or reconstruction of events. Any memory is not a true account of a happening for it is tinged by the saṃskāras of the individual that transform what the senses have received.

9. अभूतं नास्तीत्यनर्थान्तरम् ॥९।१।९॥

abhūtaṃ nāstītyanarthāntaram ॥9.1.9॥

The non-existence of what has not occurred does not explain [the presence of] a new object. 9.1.9.

This is because the non-occurring past has unlimited possibilities.

10. नास्ति घटो गेहे इति सतोघटस्य गेहसंसर्गप्रतिषथधः ॥९।१।१०॥

nāsti ghaṭo gehe iti satoghaṭasya gehasaṃsargapratiṣathadhaḥ ||9.1.10||

The absence of an object (e.g. pot) in a place is referred to as the negation of conjunction of the real (object) with the place. 9.1.10.

Statements of fact are predicated on time and they include those on absence of properties or qualities.

Perception of the Ātman

11. आत्मन्यात्ममनसोः संयोगविशेषादात्मप्रत्यक्षम् ||९|१|११||

ātmanyātmamanasoḥ saṃyogaviśeṣādātmapratyakṣam ||9.1.11||

The ātman is perceived [by the senses] when there is a particular conjunction of the ātman and mind in the ātman. 9.1.11.

The normal awareness state is outward directed with much random or chaotic activity with attention flitting from one object to another. The corresponding internal states also randomly go from one script of memory to another in a chaotic way. In these states the conjunction of the ātman and mind cannot take place.

Reflective states of concentration (dhyāna) are thus necessary to calm the vṛttis (eddies) of the mind to make it possible for the mind to obtain conjunction with the ātman.

12. तथा द्रव्यान्तरेषु प्रत्यक्षम् ॥९।१।१२॥

tathā dravyāntareṣu pratyakṣam ॥9.1.12॥

Likewise direct perception arises centered on other atomic dravyas. 9.1.12.

The direct perception of other dravyas such as atoms, ākāśa, time and space can also arise by means of the conjunction with the ātman. It is through such conjunction on the dravyas that scientists obtain their intuition.

13. असमाहितान्तः करणा उपसंहृतसमाधायस्तेषाञ्च ॥९।१।१३॥

asamāhitāntaḥ karaṇā upasaṃhṛtasamādhāyasteṣāñca ॥9.1.13॥

By those who have reached the yogic state where the mind is detached from the internal organs. 9.1.13.

The process of discovery is based on detachment from the ego and absorption in the deeper reality. This process is counterintuitive in the sense that the scientist is not obtaining the knowledge through the mind by means of a logical or inductive process but rather by withdrawing the mind and letting it obtain the insight directly from the ātman.

14. तत्समवायात् कर्मगुणेषु ॥९।१।१४॥

tatsamavāyāt karmaguṇeṣu ॥9.1.14॥

By the inherence of that (perception) in karman and attribute. 9.1.14.

The discovery requires inherence of the mind in the motions and qualities associated with the system.

15. आत्मसमवायादात्मगुणेषु ॥९।१।१५॥

ātmasamavāyādātmaguṇeṣu ॥9.1.15॥

By the inherence of ātman among the qualities of the ātman. 9.1.15.

At a deeper level, what is happening is an inherence of the ātman with qualities of the embodied ātman.

Second Āhnika

Process and Inference

1. अस्येदं कार्य्यं कारणं संयोगि विरोधि समवायि चेति लैङ्गिकम् ॥९।२।१॥

asyedaṃ kāryyaṃ kāraṇaṃ saṃyogi virodhi samavāyi ceti laiṅgikam ॥9.2.1॥

Of this [process] this activity, cause, conjunction, antagonism, inherence are the identifiers. 9.2.1.

The process of discovery requires investigation of different kinds of relationships and associations that are both constructive and antagonistic.

2. अस्येदं कार्य्यकारणसम्बन्धश्चावयवाद्भवति ॥९।२।२॥

asyedaṃ kāryyakāraṇasambandhaścāvayavādbhavati ॥9.2.2॥

"This from this" and the cause-effect relationship are of the process. 9.2.2.

The world works according to laws so causal connections must be determined.

3. एतेन शाब्दं व्याख्यातम् ॥९।२।३॥

etena śābdaṃ vyākhyātam ॥9.2.3॥

By these the knowledge [springing] from the śabda is explained. 9.2.3.

These causal connections must eventually lead to the intuition already communicated to the mind by the śabda in the ākāśa.

4. हेतुरपदेशो लिङ्गं प्रमाणं करणमित्यनर्थान्तरम् ॥९।२।४॥

heturapadeśo liṅgaṃ pramāṇaṃ karaṇamityanarthāntaram ॥9.2.4॥

Reason, etyma, signifier, proof, instrument, these all do not convey different things. 9.2.4.

Knowledge is validated by other independent means.

5. अस्येदमिति बुद्ध्यपेक्षतत्वात् ॥९।२।५॥

asyedamiti buddhyapekṣatatvāt ॥9.2.5॥

This - from this- results from the expectation of cognition. 9.2.5.

This hints at one of the paradoxes that one needs to be expecting the intuition before it can be apprehended.

Memory and Dreaming

6. आत्ममनसोः संयोगविशेषात् संस्काराञ्च स्मृतिः ॥९।२।६॥

ātmamanasoḥ saṃyogaviśeṣāt saṃskārāñca smṛtiḥ ॥9.2.6॥

The memory or recorded knowledge results from a unique conjunction of the ātman, the mind, and the stored impressions. 9.2.6.

This explains why the same event may be recalled very differently by different witnesses since their own individual stored impressions and the corresponding concentration of the mind may be different.

7. तथा स्वप्नः ॥९।२।७॥

tathā svapnaḥ ॥9.2.7॥

Likewise dreaming. 9.2.7.

In dreaming not all autobiographical memories of the conscious self are available to the ātman. Depending on what is available and what is not available the nature of the dream changes.

8. स्वप्नान्तिकम् ॥९।२।८॥

svapnāntikam ॥9.2.8॥

[And] the remembrance of the end of the dream. 9.2.8.

The remembrance of the end of the dream is also contingent on the nature of the conjunction between the ātman and the mind.

9. धर्माच्च ॥९।२।९॥

dharmācca ॥9.2.9॥

And from the substratum. 9.2.9.

This remembrance is also contingent on the very ground of the mind. Following dharma is to be consonant with existence and be in awareness whereas adharma is to go counter to the law. Therefore those who are in dharma also have a clearer understanding of the logic of the dream.

False and True Knowledge

10. इन्द्रियदोषात् संस्कारदोषाच्चाविद्या ॥९।२।१०॥

indriyadoṣāt saṃskāradoṣāccāvidyā ॥9.2.10॥

From sensory errors and and errors of habit, erroneous knowledge arises. 9.2.10.

Erroneous knowledge can also arise from false assumptions and not observing reality honestly.

11. तद्दुष्टज्ञानम् ॥९।२।११॥

tadduṣṭajñānam ॥9.2.11॥

That is false knowledge. 9.2.11.

Thus false (or defective) knowledge exists.

12. अदुष्टं विद्या ॥९।२।१२॥

aduṣṭaṃ vidyā ॥9.2.12॥

The non-erroneous is [true] knowledge. 9.2.12.

13. आर्षं सिद्धदर्शनञ्च धर्मेभ्यः ॥९।२।१३॥

ārṣaṃ siddhadarśanañca dharmebhyaḥ ॥9.2.13॥

The knowledge of the ṛṣis (sages) and the vision of the perfected ones is from the substrate (dharma). 9.2.13.

CHAPTER 10

First Āhnika

Pleasure and Pain

1. इष्टानिष्टकारणविशेषाद्विरोधाच्च मिथः सुखदुःखयोर्थान्तरभावः ॥१०।१।१॥

iṣṭāniṣṭakāraṇaviśeṣādvirodhācca mithaḥ sukhduḥkhyorthāntarabhāvaḥ ॥10.1.1॥

Desirable and non-desirable ends have particular reasons and are mutual opposites and so are pleasure and pain which are mutually different. 10.1.1.

The motivation for knowledge itself derives from a search for pleasure and, therefore, it cannot be left out of a text that purports to explain physical reality.

2. संशयनिर्णयान्तराभावाश्च ज्ञानान्तरत्वे हेतुः ॥१०।१।२॥

saṃśayanirṇayāntarābhāvāśca jñānāntaratve hetuḥ ॥10.1.2॥

Being absent in doubt and decision, and also being other than knowledge is reason. 10.1.2.

Pleasure and pain are subjective feelings that depend very much on context and expectations related to one's personal life and knowledge is different from them.

3. तयोर्निष्पत्तिः प्रत्यक्षलैङ्गिकाभ्याम् ॥१०।१।३॥

tayorniṣpattiḥ pratyakṣalaiṅgikābhyām ॥10.1.3॥

Those [doubts and decisions] arise from [errors of] perception and inference. 10.1.3.

These errors are due to the covering of ignorance. This is why bhūta-śuddhi (cleansing of the primary elements that go into forming the screen of the mind) is needed.

4. अभूदित्यपि ॥१०।१।४॥

abhūdityapi ॥10.1.4॥

From "it was", [that is, conventions] also. 10.1.4.

Conventions regarding things can also lead to feelings of pleasure and pain. Such conventions can make a person not see reason, be blind to justice and fairness, and lack compassion.

5. सति च कार्य्यादर्शनात् ॥१०।१।५॥

sati ca kāryyādarśanāt ॥10.1.5॥

In being [when senses and objects co-inhere], [pleasurable or painful] action is not seen. 10.1.5.

When senses and objects co-inhere with the ātman, objective knowledge arises that is beyond feelings of pleasure and pain.

6. एकार्थसमवायिकारणान्तरेषु दृष्टत्वात् ॥१०।१।६॥

ekārthasamavāyikāraṇāntareṣu dṛṣṭatvāt ॥10.1.6॥

[Pleasure and pain] arise from co-inherence in one [thing with different] objectives. 10.1.6.

Pleasure and pain are thus a conflation of different entities.

7. एकदेशे इत्येकस्मिन्शिरः पृष्ठमुदरं मर्माणि तद्विशेस्तद्विशेषेभ्यः ॥१०।१।७॥

ekadeśe ityekasminśiraḥ pṛṣṭhamudaram marmāṇi tadviśestadviśeṣebhyaḥ ॥10.1.7॥

One body has many parts such as the head, the stomach, the back and the vitals, and their distinctions arise from particular causes. 10.1.7.

A system -- whether the individual's physical body or a social group -- comprises of distinct sub-systems in which different kind of signals are processed.

Second Āhnika

Causality

1. कारणमिति द्रव्ये कार्य्यसमवायात् ॥१०।२।१॥

kāraṇamiti dravye kāryyasamavāyāt ॥10.2.1॥

Causation in a dravya is from inherence of action. 10.2.1.

This and the following sūtras are concerned with the nature of cause. First we speak of the inherence between the dravya and action.

2. संयोगाद्वा ॥१०।२।२॥

saṃyogādvā ॥10.2.2॥

Or from conjunction [of action]. 10.2.2.

The conjunction of the dravya and action is in the coming together of two different component dravyas.

3. कारणे समवायात् कर्माणि ॥१०।२।३॥

kāraṇe samavāyāt karmāṇi ॥10.2.3॥

When inherence in the cause, the karman [padārtha] results. 10.2.3.

Motion is then a consequence of the inherence as the cause. Thus when two dravyas with the same charge are brought together, they will move away from each other.

4. तथा रूपे कारणैकार्थसमवायाञ्च ॥१०।२।४॥

tathā rūpai kāraṇaikārthasamavāyāñca ॥10.2.4॥

And for the form [just like for other qualities], inherence of cause is the object of the action. 10.2.4.

The action is thus related to the cause in a subtle way just like the reaction that follows action in the application of force.

5. कारणसमवायात् संयोगः पटस्य ॥१०।२।५॥

kāraṇasamavāyāt saṃyogaḥ paṭasya ॥10.2.5॥

Cause inhering, [there is] conjunction with the action. 10.2.5.

Cause transfers the conjunction to action.

6. कारणकारणसमवायाञ्च ॥१०।२।६॥

kāraṇakāraṇasamavāyāñca ॥10.2.6॥

And from cause inhering in cause. 10.2.6.

A chain of causal processes is set forth.

7. संयुक्तसमवायादग्नेर्वैशेषिकम् ॥१०॥२।७॥

saṃyuktasamavāyādagnervaiśeṣikam ॥10.2.7॥

By joining the inhered, fire has distinct attribute [of heat]. 10.2.7.

The measure of heat is an aggregate of many processes.

On Authority

8. दृष्टानां दृष्टप्रयोजनानां दृष्टाभावे प्रयोगोऽभ्युयदयाय ॥१०।२।८॥

dṛṣṭānāṃ dṛṣṭaprayojanānāṃ dṛṣṭābhāve prayogo'bhyudayāya ॥10.2.8॥

Visible acts, those that are visible and purposeful, those that are not visible, are efforts for *abhyudaya* or enlightenment. 10.2.8.

The objective of the Vaiśeṣika is abhyudaya, the upliftment of all that may be taken to be the same as enlightenment.

9. तद्वचनादाम्नायस्य प्रामाण्यमिति ॥१०।२।९॥

tadvacanādāmnāyasya prāmāṇyamiti ॥10.2.9॥

Statements in the [knowledge] tradition are the proof. 10.2.9.

Knowledge is a social process and it is also validated by the experiences of others in the community. This is the reason that statements in the *āmnāya* (tradition) are valued.

PHYSICS AND FORMAL SYSTEMS AFTER KAṆĀDA

By virtue of their comprehensiveness, Kaṇāda's sūtras served as a guide for the understanding of physical and chemical phenomena in the Indic world and beyond for centuries. Their greatest influence was in the field of what would be called the principles of physics. But physics is also a mathematical system; therefore it is relevant to see how formal mathematics developed in India soon after Kaṇāda's time. We first examine the contributions of Pāṇini and Bharata Muni in their use of formal systems but we leave out the important fields of logic, mathematics, geometry, and astronomy since those contributions are well known. Further sections include the treatment of relativity of motion by Āryabhaṭa, transformation and evolution, conceptions of atoms and molecules, acoustics and music.

PĀṆINI

Pāṇini's grammar, the Aṣṭādhyāyī, described in nearly 4,000 sūtras the rules to generate all Sanskrit sentences and he collected roots in the dhātupāṭha and primitive nominal stems in the gaṇapāṭha. The Aṣṭādhyāyī is a wonderful resource for the culture and history of his times and it mentions the Naṭasūtra of Śilālin, which was the canonical text on drama in his times.

Pāṇini, by the very beauty, complexity and exhaustiveness of his rules, presaged similar efforts at complete classification in the fields of art and architecture. In this he was following an old model, in which the central results of a science are expressed in terms of sūtras, which in turn require vṛtti (turning the sutras into fully worded paraphrase) and bhāṣya (commentary) for complete explanation. Before Pāṇini's time this was already in place for the six great darśanas of Indian philosophy with their corresponding sutra texts.

Behind the rules of grammar was the idea clearly expressed in the Muṇḍaka Upaniṣad that all linguistic thought or representation can only hope to approximate reality which, in its deepest levels is transcendent (*parā*). The success of the poet and the artist owes not to the canonical rules and conventions of the medium (surface structure) but rather to the inexpressible intuition behind the conception (deep structure).

The artist strives to represent the divinity or communicate its spirit through the artistic creation, so that the aesthete might get connected to his or her own divinity within them. The beginnings of this in the Vedic ritual were in terms of representing the cosmos in the fire altar which, later, became the model for the temple, fine arts and music. Pāṇini's work falls quite within the framework of the Vedic tradition for he took the earlier Pratiśākhya rules on converting the word-for-word recitation of the Veda into a continuous recitation and created an abstract grammar of unsurpassed power.

In the Viṣṇudharmottara Purāṇa, the sage Mārkaṇḍeya says that although divinity is formless, worship and meditation are possible only when it is endowed with form. Therefore, the artist observes nature carefully and molds that inspiration using the conventions that he has internalized in the realm of his imagination.

The model for the creative sciences in India is the churning of the ocean (*samudramanthana*) that occurs within the heart of the artist. This is a dance between mechanicity and freedom, represented respectively by the demons and the gods, out of which new vision and insight emerge.

The creative process depends on rules and precepts but the artist must reach for a deeper understanding that helps him recognize the authentic and the meaningful, just as the poet cannot depend on the rules of grammar alone to find words that communicate felt experience. The driving force must thus be the transcendent self which informs the mechanistic mind.

Dākṣīputra Pāṇini was born in Śalātura in northwest India, north of the confluence of the Sindhu and the Kabul rivers. According to tradition, he became a friend of the king Mahānanda of Magadha (5th century BCE). The Kathā-sarit-sāgara of Somadeva (11th century) mentions that Pāṇini's teacher was Varṣa and his rival was Kātyāyana. The Aṣṭādhyāyī appears to supersede an earlier Aindra grammar. Xuanzang (Hieun Tsang) in the 7th century visited Śalātura and found that the grammatical tradition was continued there and that Pāṇini had been honored with a statue.

Pāṇini's grammar along with its word-lists, presents invaluable incidental information about life and society in the 5th century BCE India. It provides us names of cities, towns, villages and cultural and political entities called Janapadas, details regarding social life, economic conditions, education and learning, religion, and political conditions.The Janapada states had different kinds of government. Some Janapadas were republics, others were monarchies. We learn that the king did not have absolute power and he shared authority with his minister. This balancing of the powers created an environment that was conducive for questioning out of which emerged the many sciences that have come down to us.

Pāṇini's references shed important light on the way religion was practiced. We find that images were used to represent deities in temples and open shrines. There were images in the possession of the custodian of shrines. The Mahābhāṣya, the second century BCE commentary on Pāṇini's grammar describes temples of Dhanapati, Rāma, Kṛṣṇa, Śiva, and Viṣṇu.

Pāṇini is aware of the Vedic literature and the Upaniṣads. He also knows the Mahābhārata. Pāṇini's work is thus invaluable in the dating of the texts of the Vedic period. Pāṇini describes coins that came prior to the period of Kauṭilya's Arthaśāstra (4th century BCE). Pāṇini appears to have traveled to Pātaliputra to participate in a great annual meeting of scholars.

The structure of Pāṇini's grammar contains a meta-language, meta-rules, and other technical devices that make this system effectively equivalent to the most powerful computing machine. The other side to the discovery of this grammar is the idea that language (as a formal system) cannot describe reality completely. This limitation of language is why reality can only be experienced and never described fully.

THE NĀṬYAŚĀSTRA

What the Aṣṭādhyāyī is to language, Bharata Muni's Nāṭyaśāstra (sometimes called the fifth Veda), is to the artist and the musician. It appeared not too long after Pāṇini, classifying the diverse arts that are embodied in the classical Indian concept of the drama, including dance, music, poetics, and general aesthetics. Later, the Bṛhatsaṃhitā of Varāhamihira (505-587 CE) and the Viṣṇudharmottara Purāṇa of the 4th century CE describe canonical conventions of architecture, iconography, and painting.

The structure of Indian classical music and dance was added to by Mataṅga Muni's Bṛhaddeśi (about 600 CE), Abhinavagupta's Abhinavabhāratī and Śārṅgadeva's Sangīta Ratnākara (13th century). This connection with the tradition has continued in the Hindustani Saṅgīta Paddhati by Vishnu Nārāyaṇa Bhāṭkhaṇḍe from the early 20th century.

Bharata explains the relationship between the *bhāva*s, the emotions evoked in the spectators, and the *rasa*, essence of the performance or the work of art. He says that the artist should be conscious of the bhāva and the rasa that is being sought to be established. The word rasa itself means "juice" and it is seen as emerging from the interplay of vibhāva (stimulus that may be a word or a gesture), anubhāva (reaction) and vyabhicārī bhāva (fleeting or transitory emotion). A performance that is technically correct but has no emotion would be said to be wanting in rasa. According to Abhinavagupta, rasa is a universal mental state and the highest purpose of all creative arts is to help the connoisseur reach such a state, for the arts are the aesthetic means to knowing the self.

Bharata explains rasa by giving the parallel of the combination of various condiments, each having its own taste, which creates a unique taste that lingers. The corresponding combination in drama leads to a feeling (sthāyībhāva) that is the nāṭyarasa. In both these cases, the subject, whose mind reflects cultural and personal experience, is central to the appreciation of the creation.

The eight sthāyibhāvas are rati (love), hāsa (mirth), krodha (anger), śoka (grief), utsāha (heroism), bhaya (fear), jugupsā (disgust), and vismaya (wonder). Corresponding to these are the eight *rasas* of the Nāṭyaśāstra that form four pairs:

śṛngāra, love, devotion. Color: dark hue.

hāsya, laughter, mirth. Color: white.

raudra, fury, anger. Color: red.

kāruṇya, compassion, sadness. Color: dove colored.

vīra, heroism, courage. Color: yellowish.

bhayānaka, fear, terror. Color: dark.

bībhatsa, repulsion, aversion. Color: blue

adbhuta, wonder, astonishment. Color: yellow

The deities associated with these are Viṣṇu, Pramatha, Rudra, Yama, Indra, Kāla, Mahākala, and Brahmā, respectively. Later, the sages accepted a ninth rasa *śānta*, peace or tranquility, with the color of white and Viṣṇu as deity, and the expression *navarasa* (the nine *rasas*) became popular. Nāṭya is a sharpened representation of life wherein the various emotions are dramatically enhanced so that the spectator gains the flavor of the portrayed pleasure and pain taking him to the source of this within himself.

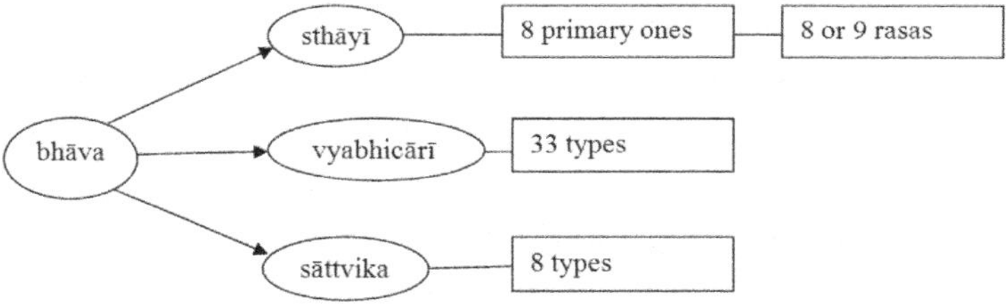

Bhāvas and rasas

There are three types of bhāva, namely sthāyī (eight types), vyabhicārī (thirty-three), and sattvika (eight), for a total of forty-nine. The eight sthāyī bhavas are the bases of the eight rasas.

The vyabhicārī bhāvas are:

nirveda (depression, caused by abuse, censure, and so on)	*glāni* (languor, result of hurt, emptiness, illness, and so on)	*śaṅkā* (suspicion)
asūyā (jealousy)	*mada* (intoxication)	*śrama* (fatigue)
ālasya (laziness)	*dainya* (misery)	*cintā* (anxiety)
moha (fainting, caused by ill luck, calamity)	*smṛti* (memory)	*dhṛti* (fortitude)
vrīḍā (sense of shame)	*capalatā* (nervousness)	*harṣa* (joy)
āvega (agitation or excitement)	*jaḍatā* (slothfulness)	*garva* (pride)
viṣāda (sorrow)	*autsukya* (unease arising from remembrance of a dear one or a beautiful place)	*nidrā* (sleepiness)
apasmāra (forgetfulness)	*supta* (overcome by sleep)	*vibodha* (awakening)
amarṣa (intolerance)	*avahittham* (dissimulation)	*ugratā* (fierceness)
mati (understanding)	*vyādhai* (illness)	*unmāda* (insanity)
maraṇam (death)	*trāsa* (dread)	*vitarka* (argumentation)

The sāttvika bhāvas are the physical manifestation of genuine emotion. They are:

stambha (stupefaction),

sveda (perspiration),

romāñca (thrill),

svarabheda (voice change),

vepathu (trembling),

vaivarṇya (facial color change),

aśru (tears),

pralaya (swoon, fainting).

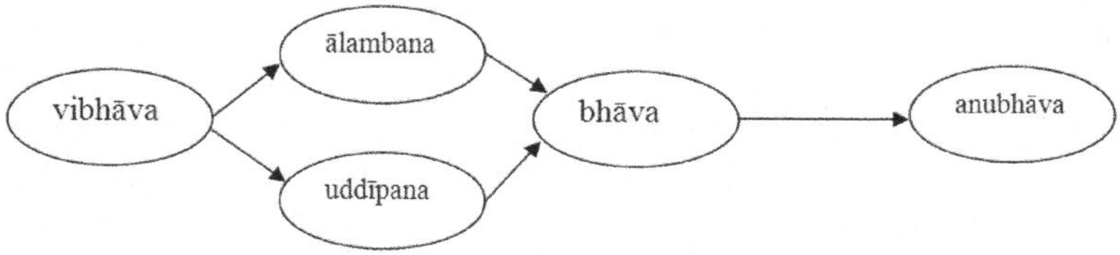

From stimulus to emotion and subsequent reaction

Vibhāva as the cause has two fundamental components: the ālambana vibhāva which is the basic stimulant and the uddīpana vibhāva which is the enhancing stimulant related to the environment and the context. If the heroine is the ālambana vibhāva, the location, like a garden, is the uddīpana vibhāva.

Abhinavagupta asks the question whether nāṭya is representation of reality (tattva) or its likeness (sadṛṣya) as in the case of a twin, or mere error (bhrānti) as in the case of silver being taken as a piece of mother-of-pearl, or superimposition (āropa), or as replica (*pratikṛti*) as in the case of a painting of a model, and so on. He asserts that nāṭya is neither of these for each of these lacks transcendence (asādhāraṇatā) without which there cannot be rasa.

The aesthetic experience is the manifestation of the innate dispositions of the self. It may be viewed as the contemplation of the bliss of the self by the connoisseur, and it is like the spiritual experience gained by the universalization that occurs during the aesthetic contemplation of characters depicted in the work of art, or in the absorption in an abstract composition.

RELATIVITY OF SPACE AND MOTION

Kaṇāda considers particular knowledge as being subjective and from there the relativity of time and space encountered in the Purāṇas and in astronomy is a small leap. Consider, for example, the specific description of relativity in the Āryabhaṭīya of the astronomer and mathematician Āryabhaṭa (born 476 CE) and it is quite conceivable that his idea that the earth spins on its axis was inspired by the symmetries inherent in the Vaiśeṣika.

Proposition 2.6 defined separations in time and space in local terms, not absolutely and it is to be expected that such relativity was employed in other scientific works. Āryabhaṭa is forced to consider the question of the relativity of motion explicitly in his explanation of the movement of the stars in the sky due to the rotation of the earth. For this, he uses the example of a boat from the perspectives of someone on it and on the shore. Āryabhaṭa declares that the shift in the perspective keeps the situation on earth unaltered as far as other processes are concerned (Shukla and Sarma, 1976).

Over a thousand years after Āryabhaṭa, Galileo presented his principle as the impossibility of using "any mechanical experiment to determine absolute uniform velocity." Although there is no comparable explicit mention of this impossibility principle in Āryabhaṭa's work, it is implicit in that the two perspectives are equivalent. Furthermore, there is explicit mention of relativity of space, and there is also mention of relativity as in the [uniform] motion of the boat, as well the [regular non-uniform] motion of the stars.

According to Āryabhaṭa, "Similar to a person in a boat moving forward who sees the stationary objects on the bank of the river as moving backwards, the stationary stars at Laṅkā (equator) are viewed as moving westwards. An illusion is created similarly that the entire structure of asterisms together with the planets is moving exactly towards the west of Laṅkā, being constantly driven by the provector wind, to cause their rising and setting."

Āryabhaṭa extends relativity of motion as experience on a boat to rotational motion of the stars, which is a significant generalization from terrestrial to astronomical phenomena. Furthermore, whereas his reference to the motion of the boat suggests uniform motion, his reference to the motion of the stars includes rotational motion.

Āryabhaṭa takes Earth as a spherical planet suspended in space surrounded by numerous stars. It is always darker on one half which is the half that is facing away from the sun and this darkness is a consequence of its own shadow. He describes how the relationship between the latitude and the time of the day varies; stating further what is clock-wise in the North Pole is anti-clockwise in the South Pole. He adds that residents of the North and the South Pole consider each other as mutually being below each other. In doing so, Āryabhaṭa is asserting the relativity of space.

Āryabhaṭa states that observers on earth do not experience their own rotational motion, observers away from the earth will detect although a westward motion. Implicitly, the laws of motion remain the same for moving objects on earth. This does sum up to the position that regular motion can be detected only by observing the system from another reference frame.

TRANSFORMATION AND EVOLUTION

The process of transformation and evolution is described conceptually in the Sāṅkhya system. The physical world is Prakṛti, which is energy in a continuum of undifferentiated qualities (guṇas), called sattva, rajas, and tamas. Sattva serves as the medium for the reflection of intelligence; rajas, energy, is characterized by a tendency to do work and overcome resistance; and tamas, mass or inertia, counteracts the energy of rajas to do work and of sattva to conscious manifestation. The infinitesimals of sattva and rajas are not material particles, but rather non-material fields.

The guṇas are always interacting with each other in different ways and it is their mutual interaction that produces the material world with its evolving structure. Seal summarizes: "The particular guṇa which happens to be predominant in any phenomenon becomes manifest in that phenomenon and the others become latent, though their presence is inferred by their effect. For example, in any material system at rest, mass is patent, energy is latent, and conscious manifestation is sub-latent…. Evolution in its formal aspect is defined as differentiation in the integrated. In other words, the process of evolution consists in the development of the differentiated within the undifferentiated, of the determinate within the indeterminate, of the coherent within the incoherent. The evolutionary series is subject to a definite law which it cannot overstep…. The guṇas, though assuming an infinite diversity of forms and powers, can neither be created nor destroyed." (Seal, 1915, pages 5-7) This conservation of guṇas is an additional principle of relevance to transformation of matter.

The Sāṅkhya evolution of matter starts with undifferentiated mass (*bhūtādi*), which is inert. Next comes tanmātra which represents subtle, vibratory matter with potential energy. Tanmātras are not atoms with specific gross properties. Rather, they are the potentials of energies represented by sound, touch, color, taste, and smell.

Vyāsa, the commentator on the Yoga Sūtra, says this about time: "Even an atom has constituent parts (tanmātras), and hence an atom must take more than one moment to change its position. The moment of that which is absolutely simple and without parts from one point in space to the next must be instantaneous, and conceived as the absolute unit of change (and therefore of time, *kṣaṇa*). If this is held to be an irreducible absolute unit, it will follow that what we represent as the time-continuum is really discrete. Time is of one dimension. Two moments cannot co-exist; neither does any series of moments exists in reality. Order in time is nothing but the relation of antecedence and sequence, between the moment that is and the moment that just went before. But only one moment, the present, exists. The future and the past have no meaning apart from potential and sub-latent phenomena.... Only one single moment is actual, and the whole universe evolves in that single moment. The rest is potential or sub-latent. (Seal, 1915, pages 19-20)

In Vyāsa's view, the sound-tanmātra, with accretion of bhūtādi, generates vibrations in ākāśa; the touch tanmātra combines with the sound-tanmātra to generate the vāyu-atom; the fire tanmātra together with the sound and touch tanmātras generates the fire-atom; the taste tanmātra together with the sound, touch, and fire tanmātras generates the water-atom; and the smell-tanmātra together with the preceding other tanmātras generates the earth-atom.

Thus, observers influence nature by the process of observation (*dṛṣṭi* in Sanskrit). This is very similar to the quantum mechanical view of the influence of observation on a physical process by the quantum Zeno effect (Kak, 2004). But the difference between quantum theory and Indian ideas is that although one speaks of observations in quantum theory there is no place in its ontology for observers. Schrödinger was aware of this limitation of quantum theory and he argued that sense-categories like the tanmātras of the Sāṅkhya system of creation at the individual or the cosmic level were essential to understand reality.

In traditional Indian art, Śiva (representing individual and universal consciousness) is shown as lifeless next to the vibrant Goddess (who represents Nature). Abstract representations of the cosmos show Śiva as a dot (of immateriality) within the (geometric) framework of the material world. Much of Indian mythology is an exposition of Indian physics in a coded language.

Indian epistemology has some parallels with Western idealism that accepts independent existence of ideas and forms. But it is different in the sense that the self has access to much more than what the individual obtains through the sense organs due to the pervasive character of the self at the individual level (*ātman*) or in its totality (*brahman*). The counter-intuitive notion of equality between the two selves makes it possible to see how large scale correlations can exist and how a person can obtain surprising insights through intuition. Naturally, such insights can only be rationalized within the framework of the individual's knowledge. Although ordinarily consciousness and matter are two distinct categories, consciousness can influence the evolution of matter through observation.

ATOMS AND MOLECULES

Atoms possess incessant vibratory motion. Heat and light rays consist of very small particles of high velocity. As material particles, their velocity is finite. This is also due to the fact that motion is contingent upon time as one of the dravyas. Heat and light particles penetrate through inter-atomic spaces, and their rays through a transparent medium get deflected or refracted. Particles of heat and light can be endowed with different characteristics and heat and light can be of different kinds. The atoms of light and heat belong to the tejas category; there are four other kinds of atoms with attributes.

There is no difference between the atom of a barley seed and paddy seed, for both these are constructed out of the atoms of earth. Under the impact of heat particles, atoms exhibit new characteristics. A *bhūta*-atom evolves out of integration from the corresponding *tanmātra*, which is its potential form, indicating a primacy of the abstract over the material. Although atoms are unitary objects their combinations generate various tanmātras. Combinations of rudiment-matter (*bhūtādi*) lead to more specific forms. The vibrations of atoms increase and change when acted upon by energy. Every molecule contains at least one atom of all four types, and obtains its character from the predominance of a given element. This makes it possible to see how molecules may show characteristics of more than one element and they might also burn or become liquid.

The atom's potentiality manifests in distinct attributes based on state of conjunction and motion. It is this potentiality that leads to diverse complex atoms with different attributes. These attributes may be viewed as being created by the matrix of space, time and number. Light has a special place in this view as it is both an elementary constituent of matter as well as the medium that shines the inner space of the mind. The atom of light cannot be described fully.

To conceive positions in space, Vācaspati Miśra takes three axes: one from east to west, second from north to south, and a third up to the meridian position of the sun, anticipating three-dimensional solid geometry. He speaks of a lattice arrangement of atoms where each is in contact with six others.

Ākāśa has no atomic structure and is inert, being posited only as the substratum of sound, which is supposed to travel wave-like in the manifesting medium or vehicle of vāyu. Pṛthivī, āpas, tejas, and vāyu atoms are possessed of characteristic properties of mass, fluidity, and so on. These atoms unite in atomic or molecular forms.

One atom may combine with another to form a binary molecule with inherent *parispanda* (rotational or vibrational motion). The binary molecules combine by threes, fours, fives, and so on to form larger aggregates and a variety of elementary substances.

A triad holds together three atoms, not three binary molecules. An elementary substance may suffer qualitative change under the influence of heat particles. One scholar (Gaṅgeśa) suggests that even gold can evaporate by application of intense heat. Chemical combination takes place either between two or more substances that are isomeric modifications of the same bhūta, or between substances which are modes of different bhūtas.

Praśastapāda describes a scheme in which molecules combine to form a compound (Figure 4). The atom's potentiality manifests in distinct attributes based on state of conjunction and motion. It is this potentiality that leads to diverse complex atoms with different attributes. These attributes may be viewed as being created by the matrix of space, time and number. The forces are mediated by atoms of one kind or the other.

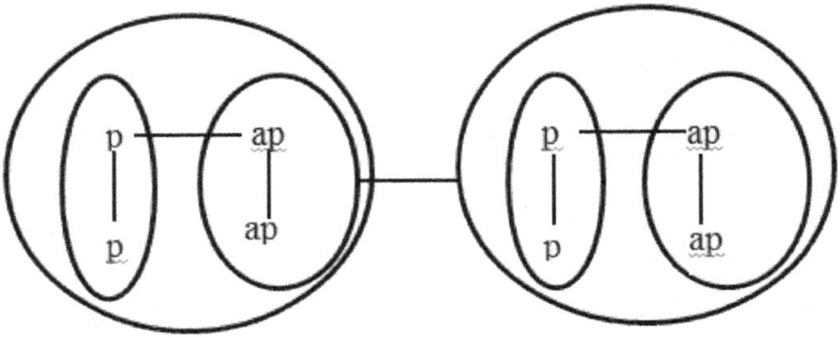

Molecules of a compound (p=earth atom; ap=water atom)
(after Seal, 1915)

Other scholars argue that for two atoms to come together to form a molecule, the linkages between the two should be in terms of attraction based on opposite attributes. Electricity and magnetism as well as light were seen to be a property of tejas atoms.

ACOUSTICS AND MUSIC

In their analysis of sound, the Indian tradition distinguishes between three types: *nāda, dhvani,* and *sphoṭa*. Nāda is the physical basis of sound, dhvani is the audible sound, and sphoṭa is the idea behind the sound. Śabara (c. 300) and Kumārila Bhaṭṭa (c. 700) of the Mīmāṃsā School speak clearly of how the vibration of collections of air molecules produces audible sound. Bhartṛhari (5th century) in his Vākyapadīya describes sounds as arising out of the pressure waves related to variations in velocity and configuration.

The vibrating air molecules at the source of the sound suffer a deviation from their usual motion that generates a saṃskāra which transfers this vibration to neighboring molecules in succession so that the sound wave travels out and the energy of this dissipates with distance. Such a saṃskāra may be viewed from the perspectives of elasticity as well as momentum from an impressed force. Some writers state that elasticity is one of the causes of vibration and it resides in all the four atomic elements (earth, water, fire, air). Such elastic property will explain how sound can travel in solids and liquids.

Echo (*pratidhvani*) was seen in the same manner as image in a mirror (*pratibimba*). Sounds differ from one another in their pitch (*tāramandādibheda*), intensity (*tīvramandādibheda*), and timbre (*asādhāraṇa dharma*).

In one view, cosmic sound as nāda is the cause of the material universe and it is identified with the Brahman of the Upaniṣads. Nāda is synonymous with parā vāk, and it comes in two forms: āhata (perceptible sound), and anāhata (unstuck or absolute sound). Music is the elevated form of āhata nāda whereas anāhata nāda can be cognized only through Yoga.

Indian musical tests tell us that 22 śrutis span the seven notes of the octave. In the Shadjagrāma scale, the seven notes are at intervals of 4, 3, 2, 4, 4, 3, 2 śrutis, and it is not clear why the division is into groups of four, three, and two into the seven musical notes (Nijenhuis, 1974). It is possible that the division began with equal śrutis, to the extent possible) and the notes were shifted somewhat to provide richness. It was known that the pitch of a note is inversely proportional to the length of the wire. It was known that the pitch of the fundamental note to that of its octave is 1:2, that of the fourth to the fundamental is 4:3, and that of the fifth to the fundamental is 3:2.

EPILOGUE

The examination of the various parts of the Vaiśeṣika system reveals that its observables arise through the effect of motion of atoms in a consistent manner. Although the moderns with their knowledge of contemporary sciences might quibble with the framework of the Vaiśeṣika, it offers a comprehensive and scientific view of the universe beginning with gross visible matter all the way up to the subtle invisible mind. Specifically, it deals with motion, laws and symmetries, atoms and molecules, transformations and evolution. It argues that molecules can inter-transform and amongst the effects it describes is that of electricity and magnetism for it presumed that the tejas atoms were at the basis of the electric and magnetic phenomena.

The atom is indivisible because it is a state for which no measurement can be attributed. What cannot be measured cannot be further divided and it cannot be spoken of as having parts. The motion the atom possesses is non-observable and it may be viewed as an abstraction in a conventional sense. Space and time are the two lenses through which matter is observed and they form the matrix of universe. The distinction between intrinsic and extrinsic motions arises from the fact that intrinsic motion is uniform in all directions.

When the universe ceases to be at the end of the cosmic cycle, the transmuted matter reaches a quiescent state in which there is no extrinsic motion and so it becomes invisible; this appears very similar to the conception of the state of the aggregate of atoms at the beginning of cycle of creation. The lack of motion represents a cessation of time, because time is a measure of change.

In the epistemology of the Vaiśeṣika system, it is possible to obtain knowledge due to the agency of ātman or self. It is striking that the Vaiśeṣika is of contemporary interest for it includes observers and the idea of consciousness. Modern physics has grappled with the problem of observers, but without much success, as attempts to see consciousness as emerging out of complexity of neural structures do not explain why and how it emerges.

The six ontological categories of the Vaiśeṣika include three for the outer reality (based on substance, qualities, and motion as in standard physics) and three more for the intuitive space associated with the interaction of the observer with the physical system. This second set of three categories of the universal, the particular, and inherence between the senses of the observer and the physical system take into account the qualia that must form the foundation for our understanding of the physical reality. By doing so, Kaṇāda brilliantly accounts for the working of consciousness through the agency of the mind.

Scientists are generally agreed that the absence of sentient observers in the conception of science means that it is an incomplete picture. The consideration of minds and consciousness as a starting point of the Vaiśeṣika system is conceptually attractive. In principle these categories can be formally studied in physics and there is the promise that it will lead to verifiable or falsifiable predictions.

The ideas of the Vaiśeṣika can also be of important in the study of neuroscience and models of consciousness.

NOTES

INTRODUCTION

For a general overview of the Vedic system of knowledge, see Kak (2015) and Kak (2016a), where the former provides a general overview of the epistemology and the latter an account of Vedic astronomy. The author's earlier contribution to the Vaiśeṣika was Kak (2001) and his comparative studies of logic and science include Kak (2004) and Kak (2009).

The scientific ideas of the Vedic tradition have had much influence on the Western sciences. Indian mathematics has influenced world mathematics in a profound way in the adoption of the Indian number system, and by its many methods for the solution of geometric, arithmetic and algebraic problems that were spread to Europe by Arabic intermediaries. The notion of a formal generative system in the manner of Pāṇini's grammar has influenced not only mathematical thought but also other disciplines that include comparative and historical linguistics.

A SUMMARY OF THE VAIŚEṢIKA SYSTEM

The text followed in this book is from Śāstri (2002). For general overview of the Vaiśeṣika, see Matilal (1977), Potter (1997) and Kumar (2013).

PHYSICS AND FORMAL SYSTEMS AFTER KAṆĀDA

For Pāṇini's contributions, see Cardona (1997) and Sharma (2001); for the Nāṭyaśāstra, see Ghosh (1967). For a discussion of the history and philosophy of ideas of physics and cognitive science see Kak (2016b) and Kak (2016c).

Indian mathematical ideas accompanied the spread of Buddhism into China in early centuries CE. The translations of Āryabhaṭa's Āryabhaṭīya as Arajbahar, Brahmagupta's BSS as Zij al-Sindhind and his Khaṇḍakhādyaka as Arkand had far-reaching influence on Arabic works and through them on European astronomy and mathematics. The Arabic scholar al-Khwarizmi (c. 780-850 CE) is known to have written two works, one based on Indian astronomy (Zij) and the other on Indian arithmetic (possibly Kitāb al-Adad al-Hindi). A Latin translation of this second work "The Book of Hindu Reckoning" (Algorithmi De Numero Indorum) was made in Spain around the 11th century. This book and Fibonacci's Liber Abaci (Book of Calculation) that appeared in 1202 spread Indian numerals into Europe.

The inability of the framework of modern physics to account for the observer has been stressed by many physicists including Schrödinger (1967) and Penrose (2004). The creators of quantum theory sidestepped the problem of consciousness using the philosophical view of psychophysical parallelism. According to Moritz Schlick, who was the leader of the Vienna Circle of Logical Positivists in the 1930s, psychophysical parallelism is the "epistemological parallelism between psychological conceptual system on the one hand and a physical conceptual system on the other. The 'physical world' is just the world that is designated by means of the system of quantitative concepts of the natural sciences." (Schlick, 1918/1974) This idea in Europe goes back to Leibnitz.

Neils Bohr stressed the elusive separation between subject and object:

> The epistemological problem under discussion may be characterized briefly as follows: For describing our mental

> activity, we require, on one hand, an objectively given content to be placed in opposition to a perceiving subject, while, on the other hand, as is already implied in such an assertion, no sharp separation between object and subject can be maintained, since the perceiving subject also belongs to our mental content. (Bohr, 1929)

The principle of psychophysical parallelism is consistent with complementarity and indeed the inspiration for it. Bohr argued that the consideration of the biological counterpart to the observation of the relation between mind and body does not become part of an infinite regress. He argued that "We have no possibility through physical observation of finding out what in brain processes corresponds to conscious experience. An analogy to this is the information we can obtain concerning the structure of cells and the effects this structure has on the way organic life displays itself.... What is complementary is not the idea of a mind and a body but that part of the contents of the mind which deals with the ideas of physics and the organisms and that situation where we bring in the thought about the observing subject." (Bohr, 2013)

In the standard view of physics or neuroscience, humans can have no freedom. Nevertheless, freedom is felt intuitively by every person. The Vaiśeṣika takes the problem of freedom or agency head on and resolves it by invoking the ātman in a manner that is entirely consistent with other Vedic philosophical systems. In considering the physical and the mental as forming separate ontological categories, it is consistent with psyhophysical parallelism behind the Copenhagen Interpretation of quantum theory.

BIBLIOGRAPHY

Balasubramaniam, R. and Joshi, J.P. (2008). Analysis of terracotta scale of Harappan civilization from Kalibangan. Current Science, vol. 95, pp. 588-589.

Bishagratna, K.K.L. (ed.) (1907). The Sushruta Samhita. Calcutta.

Bohr, N. (1929). Wirkungsquantum und Naturbeschreibung. Die Naturwissenschaften 17, 483–486

Bohr, N. (2013). Complementarity beyond Physics. Elsevier.

Burgess, E. (1860). The Sūrya Siddhānta. Motilal Banarsidass, Delhi, 1989.

Cardona, G. (1997). Panini: His Work and Its Traditions. Motilal Banarsidass, Delhi

Chakrabarty, D. (2003). Vaiśeṣika Sūtra of Kaṇāda. DK Printworld.

Danino, M. (2008). New insights into Harappan town-planning, proportions and units, with special reference to Dholavira. Man and Environment, vol. 33, No. 1, pp. 66-79.

Elliot, H.M. and Dowson, J. (1867). The History of India, as Told by Its Own Historians. London.

Ganguly, K.M. (tr.) (1990). The Mahābhārata. Munshiram Manoharlal, New Delhi.

Ghosh, M. (1967). The Nāṭyaśāstra. Manisha Granthalaya, Calcutta.

Halbfass, W. (1992). On Being and What There Is: Classical Vaiśeṣika and the History of Indian Ontology. State University of New York Press.

Kak, S. (2001). Physical concepts in the Sāṅkhya and Vaiśeṣika systems. In Life, Thought and Culture in India, G.C. Pande (ed.). Centre for Studies in Civilizations, 413-437.

Kak, S. (2004). The Architecture of Knowledge. CSC and Motilal Banarsidass, New Delhi.

Kak, S. (2009). Logic in Indian thought. In: Schumann A (ed.) Logic in religious discourse. Ontos Verlag, Frankfurt.

Kak, S. (2015). The Wishing Tree. Aditya Prakashan, New Delhi.

Kak, S. (2016a). The Astronomical Code of the Ṛgveda. Aditya Prakashan, New Delhi.

Kak, S. (2016b). The Nature of Physical Reality. Mount Meru Publishing, Mississauga, Canada.

Kak, S. (2016c). Mind and Self: Patañjali's Yoga Sūtra and Modern Science. Mount Meru Publishing, Mississauga, Canada.

Kumar, S.P. (2013). Classical Vaiśeṣika in Indian Philosophy. Routledge, London.

Larson, G.J. and R.S. Bhattacharya (ed.) (1987). Sāṃkhya: A Dualist Tradition in Indian Philosophy. Princeton University Press, Princeton.

Matilal, B.K. (1977). Nyāya-Vaiśeṣika. Otto Harrasowitz, Wiesbaden.

Moore W (1989). Schrödinger: life and thought. Cambridge University Press.

Morley, I. and Renfrew, C. (eds.) (2010). The Archaeology of Measurement. Cambridge University Press.

Nijenhuis, E. (1974). Indian Music: History and Structure. E.J. Brill, Leiden.

Nikhilananda, Swami (1953). Vivekananda: The Yogas and Other Works. Ramakrishna-Vivekananda Center, New York.

Penrose, R. (2004). The Road to Reality. Vintage, New York.

Potter, K.H. (1997). Indian Metaphysics and Epistemology: The Tradition of Nyāya-Vaiśeṣika up to Gaṅgeśa. Delhi.

Prasad, R. (1912). Patañjali's Yoga Sutras. Panini Office, Prayaga.

Ray, P.C. (1909). A History of Hindu Chemistry. Vols. I & II. London: Williams and Norgate.

Śāstri, Ḍhunḍirāja (2002). Vaiśeṣikasūtropaskāra of Śaṅkara Miśra. Chaukhambha Prakashan, Varanasi.

Schlick, M. (1918/1974). General Theory of Knowledge. Springer.

Schrödinger, E. (1967) What is Life? and Mind and Matter. Cambridge University Press, Cambridge.

Seal, B. (1915). The Positive Sciences of the Hindus. Motilal Banarsidass, Delhi, 1985.

Sharma, R. (2001). Aṣṭādhyāyī of Pāṇini. Munshiram Manoharlal, New Delhi.

Shukla, K.S. and Sarma, K.V. (1976). Āryabhaṭīya of Āryabhaṭa. Indian National Science Academy, New Delhi.

Tewari, R. (2003). The origins of iron working in India: New evidence from the Central Ganga plain and the Eastern Vindhyas. Antiquity, 77: 536-544.

Vidyabhusana, S.C. (1990). The Nyāya Sūtras of Gotama, revised and edited by Nandalal Sinha. Motilal Banarsidass, Delhi.

INDEX

Made in United States
Orlando, FL
14 March 2022

15775614R00124